25' TRANSPORTABLE PORT SECURITY BOAT OPERATOR'S HANDBOOK

COMDTINST M16114.34

U.S. Department of
Homeland Security

United States
Coast Guard

I0447348

U.S. Department of Homeland Security

United States Coast Guard

Commandant
United States Coast Guard

2100 Second Street, SW
Washington, DC 20593-0001
Staff Symbol: G-OPD
Phone: 202-267-2039

COMDTINST M16114.34
27 October 2003

COMMANDANT INSTRUCTION M16114.34

Subj: 25' TRANSPORTABLE PORT SECURITY BOAT OPERATOR'S HANDBOOK

1. <u>PURPOSE</u>. This Manual provides technical orientation, performance characteristics, and basic operating procedures for the 25' Transportable Port Security Boat. It also standardizes boat outfit equipment and layout.

2. <u>ACTION</u>. Area and district commanders, commanders of maintenance and logistics commands, commanding officers of headquarters units, and assistant commandants for directorates, Chief Counsel, special staff offices at Headquarters, and Port Security Unit (PSU) commanding officers shall ensure compliance with the provisions of this Manual. Internet release is authorized.

3. <u>DIRECTIVES AFFECTED</u>. None.

4. <u>DISCUSSION</u>. This Manual contains the information necessary to safely and efficiently operate the 25' Transportable Port Security Boat. The operational capabilities, limitations, and emergency procedures are clearly stipulated. The fittings, outfit list, and physical characteristics of the boat are pictured and described in detail. This Manual is directive in nature and applies to all 25' Transportable Port Security Boat crews, operational commanders.

5. <u>PROCEDURE</u>. Area, operational and unit commanders for all 25' Transportable Port Security Boat units shall ensure the procedures and limitations detailed in this manual are followed. Forward any comments, corrections, recommendations and questions regarding this handbook to the PSU Program Manager per Chapter One of this Manual.

6. <u>ENVIRONMENTAL CONSIDERATIONS</u>. Pollution prevention considerations were examined in the development of the Manual and have been determined to be not applicable.

DISTRIBUTION – SDL No. 140

	a	b	c	d	e	f	g	h	i	j	k	l	m	n	o	p	q	r	s	t	u	v	w	x	y	z
A																										
B		1	1						1			1		1												
C					1						1		1		1									1		
D				1																						
E																										
F																										
G			2	1	2																					
H																										

NON-STANDARD DISTRIBUTION:

7. <u>FORMS AVAILABILITY</u>. U.S. Coast Guard Training Record (CG-5285), Stockpoint: SCB, Stock Number: 7530-01-GF2-9980, Unit of Description: Folder, Unit of Issue: Each. Administrative Remarks (CG-3307), Small Arms Record Firing Report (CG-3029), Unit training Plan (CG-5293), Coast Guard Mission Area Formal School Record (CG-5396), Coxswain Certificate (CG-5063), Boat Engineer Certificate (CG-5063A), Boat Crewmember Certificate (CG-5063B), are available on the standard workstation in JetForm Filler and Adobe Forms.

D. S. BELZ /s/
Assistant Commandant for Operations

RECORD OF CHANGES			
CHANGE NUMBER	DATE OF CHANGE	DATE ENTERED	BY WHOM ENTERED

Table of Contents

CHAPTER 1   INTRODUCTION

CHAPTER 2   BOAT CHARACTERISTICS

CHAPTER 3   BOAT SYTEMS AND COMPONENTS

CHAPTER 4   THE CREW

CHAPTER 5   BOAT OPERATIONS

CHAPTER 6 MISSION PERFORMANCE

CHAPTER 7 EMERGENCY PROCEDURES/ CASUALTY CONTROL

APPENDIX

CHAPTER 1 INTRODUCTION

Overview

Introduction	This handbook outlines safety and operational procedures for the Coast Guard's 25' Transportable Port Security Boat (TPSB). It clearly defines operational capabilities, limitations, and emergency procedures. This manual describes the 25' TPSB systems in terms of purpose, operation and maintenance. In addition, it shows or describes the boats fittings, outfit list, and physical characteristics of the boat.		
In this chapter			
	Section	**Topic**	**See Page**
	A	Warnings, Cautions, and Notes	1-3
	B	Platform Management	1-3
	C	Changes	1-3
	D	Action	1-4

THIS PAGE INTENTIONALLY LEFT BLANK

	Section A: Warnings, Cautions, And Notes
A.1. General	The following definitions apply to Warnings, Cautions, and Notes found throughout the handbook.
A.2. WARNING 🖐	**Operating procedures or techniques that must be carefully followed to avoid personal injury or loss of life.**
A.3. CAUTION!	**Operating procedures or techniques that must be carefully followed to avoid equipment damage**
A.4. NOTE ⌒	**Operating procedures or techniques that must be carefully followed to avoid equipment damage**

	Section B: Platform Management
B.1. Commandant (G-OPD)	Commandant (G-OPD) is the platform manager for the 25' TPSB. The TPSB is a standard boat as defined in the Boat Management Manual, COMDTINST M16114.4 (series), and the Naval Engineering Manual, COMDTINST M9000.6 (series).
B.2. Special Missions Training Center (SMTC)	Commandant (G-WTT) provides support to Commandant (G-OPD) via Headquarters program oversight of the Coast guard Special missions Training Center (SMTC), located at the Marine Corps Base Camp Lejeune, NC. SMTC provides expertise directly to field units regarding the effective operation and maintenance of the TPSB as well as platform standardization team functions. SMTC will generally be the site chosen to evaluate proposed alterations or new equipment/policies.

	Section C: Changes
C.1. General	Commandant (G-OPD) is the program manager for Port Security Units and promulgates this manual and its changes. Submit recommendations for corrections or changes to Commandant (G-OPD) via standard letter or electronic mail. The address and phone number for (G-OPD) is as follows: COMMANDANT (G-OPD) 2100 2ND STREET SW WASHINGTON, DC 20593-0001 (202) 267-2039
C.2. Engineering Changes	Appendix A is an index of all approved Engineering Changes issued since the 25' TPSB has been in service. ECs issued after the date of this revision supersede information in this manual where applicable.

	Section D: Action
D.1. General	Units, operational commanders, and boat crews will comply with the procedures and limitations specified in this publication and any duly issued changes.
NOTE⚬	**To maintain fleet-wide standardization, unit commanders are not authorized to change or vary the type or location of equipment carried except where noted. Design or structural alterations are prohibited unless specifically authorized by the Office of Naval Engineering, Commandant (G-SEN). Prototype testing of 25' TPSB configuration changes may only be carried out with the specific authorization of the Office of Naval Engineering, Commandant (G-SEN). SMTC will generally be chosen to evaluate proposed alterations or new equipment/policies**

CHAPTER 2 BOAT CHARACTERISTICS	
Overview	
Introduction	This chapter describes the standard 25' TPSB features and equipment. A detailed description of each system is found in **Chapter 3**, **Boat Systems and Components**. Where discrepancies exist, commands shall initiate action to comply with these standards. All illustrations in this handbook are for familiarization purposes only. The placement of machinery and equipment depicted in illustrations may not reflect the current proper placement and installation of equipment and machinery. Refer to the appropriate blueprint, technical publication or enclosure to this handbook for the latest proper placement.
NOTE	**Be aware of and allow for any differences in a particular boat as compared to the standard measurements, particularly with regard to maximum operating height above water (i.e., antennas).**
In this chapter	

	Section	Topic	See Page
	A	General Description	2-3
	B	Hull	2-5
	C	Trailer	2-7
	D	Nomenclature	2-9

THIS PAGE INTENTIONALLY LEFT BLANK

Section A: General Description	
A.1. Manufacturer	The 25' Transportable Port Security Boat (TPSB) is a twin outboard, open deck, all weather, high performance, moderately armed platform capable of operating in inner harbor/near shore environments in light sea conditions. It was first built in FY97 by Boston Whaler in Edgewater, Florida, for the US Coast Guard, Maintenance and Logistic Command.
A.2. Missions	The 25' TPSB is designed and configured to support PSUs as an inshore/harbor surface interdiction response asset in accordance with Required Operational Capabilities (ROC) and Projected Operational Environment (POE) for Coast Guard Port Security Units (PSU), COMDTINST 3501.49 (series).
A.3. Design	The basic design is based on the standard Boston Whaler 25' Guardian hull, customized to functionally suit the TPSB mission requirements. The basic craft arrangements consist of a centrally positioned control console and leaning post with an open work deck and low non-obstructive gunwhales. The TPSB is outfitted as a military gunboat with three (3) hardened weapon positions: (1) forward .50 cal tri-pod, (2) gunwhale - mounted 7.62mm M240B Machine Gun pipe pedestals, port and starboard.
A.4. Boat Specification	Page 2-4 lists the standard 25' TPSB boat specifications.

Characteristic	Specification
Length (On Trailer Engines Tilted Up)	24' 07" (37 0")
Beam (On trailer)	8' 0" (9' 0")
Draft (Boat Only) (Engines Down)	(1' 04") (3' 03")
Maximum speed	50 Knots/ 32 Knots with full load
Engines	Evenrude 175 hp FICHT
Horsepower, each engine	175
Maximum horsepower	450
Fuel	87 Octane unleaded gasoline
Fuel capacity	171.3 gallons
VRO capacity	(2) 2.5 gallons
Propellers	Two, 3-bladed stainless, 17" pitch
Transom Height	30"
Boat weight (empty hull)	3575 lbs
Boat weight (complete outfit)	5320 lbs
Total weight (persons, engines, gear) that boat will support	9000 lbs
Underway crew endurance	8 hours out of 24
Operating sea conditions	Designed to operate in condition of Sea state 3 (3.5 to 5 ft wave height). Fully capable when operating in less than 2 ft seas and under 30 knots of wind. TPSB may operate in up to 6 ft seas with a degraded mission capability.
Operating wind conditions	Winds up to 30 knots
Max personnel capacity	12

Section B: Hull

B.1. Description	The hull is made of a fiberglass foam core construction. The inner and outer skins of fiberglass are joined with a closed cell, high-density foam that chemically bonds the two skins completely together. The high-density foam fills all voids between the two skins to form a solid, one-piece, lightweight hull finished with a gray dyed gel coat.
	The hull incorporates a forward anchor locker, a forward below-deck stowage cavity, a centerline fuel tank cavity and molded-in rigging troughs. The cockpit floor consists of two removable fiberglass composite panels; one panel covers the forward stowage cavity and the second panel covers the fuel tank and rigging troughs. The panels are fastened in place with stainless steel screws. The screws are threaded into aluminum inserts molded into the hull interior. The perimeter of each panel is sealed with RTV silicone. For additional support, the floor panels are supported by aluminum beams. The console and leaning posts are fastened directly to the floor panels with machine screws into aluminum inserts that are molded into the panels.
	Wood, phenolic and/or aluminum inserts are molded into the hull for mounting hardware and accessories. It is important that accessories be located in a safe position and installed so that they will remain securely in place. Accessories subject to heavy loading and high stresses, such as handrails and cleats, should only be installed in areas that have been reinforced with additional laminate and inserts. Thru-bolting with backing plates is often the most secure way to install equipment where access is available.
	In order to prevent water from seeping under or behind a newly installed accessory, it is important to coat the contact surface with a marine grade sealant or adhesive. In the event an accessory is removed from the boat it is important that the fastener holes be sealed immediately.
B.2. Equipment	Appendix D lists the equipment and hardware that is standard outfit on the 25' TPSB hull:
B.3. Hull Maintenance **B.3.1. General**	To ensure that the hull will provide the maximum amount of service life and to maintain it in good condition, the following care and maintenance will be taken: <ul><li>Washing</li><li>Waxing</li><li>Compounding</li><li>Repairs of damaged gel-coat surfaces</li><li>Trim Care</li></ul>

B.3.2. Washing	Exterior and interior gel-coat and metal hardware will be washed down after each tour of duty using fresh water, a mild soap, and clean cloths or a sponge. **Do not use** abrasive cleaners, abrasive pads, steel or bronze wool, or alkaline cleaners. After washing, rinse thoroughly with fresh water. Dry to prevent water spots from forming on the hull and bright work.
B.3.3. Waxing	The exterior and interior surfaces and deck should be waxed a minimum of twice per year to protect the gel coat from salt, dirt, and ultraviolet (UVA/UVB) degradation. Use a wax that has been specifically formulated for fiberglass and gel coated parts. Do not use automotive products, as they will not provide the required protection. Follow the manufacturers instructions. Do not wax the hull in direct sunlight. The gel-coat could "haze" over if waxed in direct sunlight or high temperature.
B.3.4. Compounding	On occasion, it may be necessary to compound the gel-coat to remove stains, light scratches, oxidation and hazed films. Compounding should only be done after the boat has been thoroughly cleaned to remove all dirt and oil. Use a fine grade compound formulated for fiberglass and gel-coated parts. Follow the manufacturer's instructions carefully. After compounding, re-wax all surfaces.
B.3.5. Surface Repairs	Minor scratches can often be compounded out after washing. Deeper gel-coat scratches may have to be wet sanded out. This should only be done with 400 to 600 grit wet/dry sandpaper. Fiberglass and gel coat repair work should only be done by trained personnel. Any gel-coat repair should be done with gel-coat that has a haze gray color component added to it.

Section C: Trailer

C.1. Description	The 25' TPSB is accompanied by a 10,000 lbs G.V.W. (Gross Vehicle Weight) galvanized trailer. The trailer is manufactured by Loadrite Trailers Inc. (B.W. #G5-9400-25). It has been designed to withstand the unusual demands placed upon it through military service. The trailer design is specific to the 25' TPSB, ensuring proper hull support, balance and safety. The trailer is constructed of heavy wall tubular chassis and cross member. Each of the structural components of the trailer are hot-dipped galvanized to resist the corrosive and weathering effects of the environment.
C.2. Specifications	Load Capacity 8,000 LBS G. V. W. Rating 10,000 LBS Weight 2,000 LBS Tire Size 8/14.5 F Number of Axles 2 Chassis Size 3" X 6" Overall Length 27' 5" Overall Width 9 ft Number of Keel Rollers 8 Number of Keel Guide Bunks 2 Number of Float on Guides 2 Number of Roller Trains 2 Winch Capacity 3,200 LBS Winch Line Type Wire or strap

C. 3. Standard Equipment	The following equipment and hardware is standard on the 25' trailer
	(2) Plastic coated safety wires with shackles Hydraulic surge brakes Galvanized axles Galvanized wheel rims Stoltz keel rollers 6" Keel guide bunks Roller train Float on side guides Front and rear fender step pads Movable undercarriage Waterproof tail and marker lights Heavy duty winch Caster Jack Brake flush kit Welded on spare tire carrier Tie down straps Spare tire with rim. Mounted on spare tire carrier. Dual caster wheels with inflatable tires (2) High lift kit for loading into aircraft Interchangeable Pintle and Ball hitches Boxes mounted on trailer aft of tongue
C.4. Maintenance	Inspection. Conduct pre-operational inspections of the trailer components to determine the following: The correct tire pressure as specified is present in the tires. • Each of the roller train rollers rotate freely. • The winch wire is not frayed or damaged in any way. • The brake flush fittings and hoses are free of obstructions. • The keel rollers rotate freely and are not torn. • The tail lights are sealed and operate properly. • The electrical wiring is free of damage and corrosion. • The keel guide bunks are not damaged and the carpet covering is not torn. • The float on guides are not damaged and the carpet covering is not torn. • Fasteners are properly tighten and free of corrosion or damage. Maintenance. After each launch and each retrieval of the 25' TPSB, the trailer components, including the brakes, should be rinsed/flushed with fresh water. Periodic maintenance of the trailer and its components should be performed IAW manfacturer's recommendations.

Section D: Nomenclature

Bow

The M2 .50 Cal machine gun mount is located in the bow, directly over the forward void.

D.1. .50 Caliber Machine Gun Mount	The tripod mount is used in conjunction with the Mk 93 Mod 0 machine gun mount
D.2. Eye Bolt	The trailer eyebolt is backed with a steel plate and two bolts.
D.3. Cleat	The forward cleat is located on the bow of the boat.

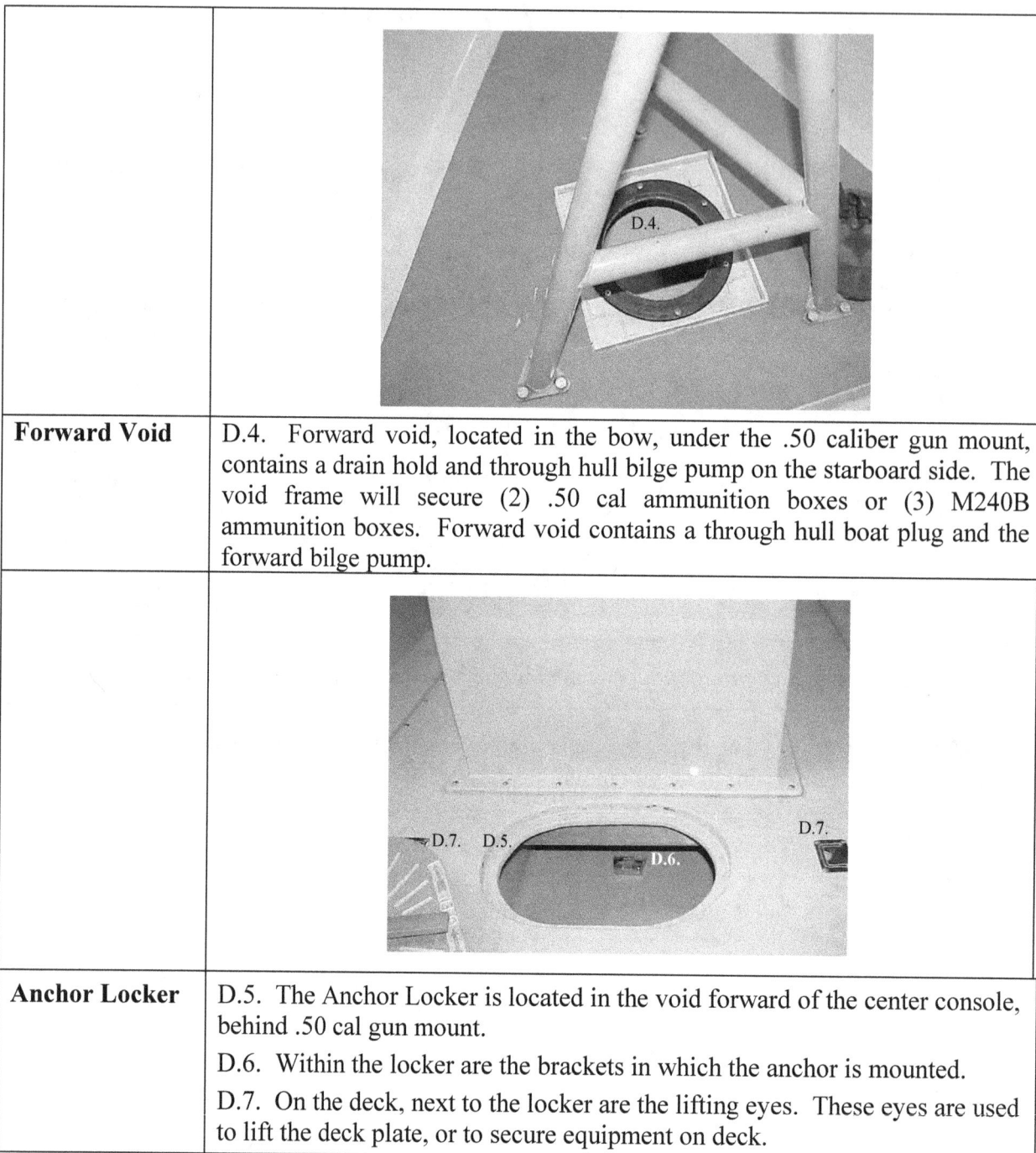

Forward Void	D.4. Forward void, located in the bow, under the .50 caliber gun mount, contains a drain hold and through hull bilge pump on the starboard side. The void frame will secure (2) .50 cal ammunition boxes or (3) M240B ammunition boxes. Forward void contains a through hull boat plug and the forward bilge pump.
Anchor Locker	D.5. The Anchor Locker is located in the void forward of the center console, behind .50 cal gun mount. D.6. Within the locker are the brackets in which the anchor is mounted. D.7. On the deck, next to the locker are the lifting eyes. These eyes are used to lift the deck plate, or to secure equipment on deck.

Center Console	
	D.8. Center Console D.9. Blue Light D.10. Blue Light and Siren
Center Console Compartment	
Port Side Center Console	
	D.11. Center Console Compartment Access, Port side. D.12. The Fire Extinguisher Mount is located outside the compartment. D.13. Port Side console handrail.

Starboard Side Center Console	
	D.13. Starboard Side console handrail. D.14. Center Console Compartment Access, starboard side. Contains the breaker box and searchlight. Inside the starboard console are 3 - 12 volt batteries: 1 for each engine and 1 for the electrical system. The interior starboard side of the console holds a 50' shore tie electrical cord and the battery charger.
Breaker Box	
	• D.15. PRC 117 Breaker • D.20. Radar Breaker • D.16. Spectra Radio Breaker • D.21. Radio 2 Breaker • D.17. Spare Breaker • D.22. Radio 3 Breaker • D.18. Depth finder Breaker • D.23. Main Breaker • D.19. GPS Breaker • D.24. Search Light

Center Console Instrument Panel

Center Console Switches

- D.25. GPS
- D.26. GPS Sensor
- D.27. Compass
- D.28. PRC 117 Mount
- D.29. Speaker
- D.30 Depth Finder

- D.31. - D.32. VRO Gauges port/stbd
- D.41. FM Radio
- D.33. - D.34. Water Temp Gauges port/stbd
- D.35. Radar
- D.36. - D.37. Tachometer port/stbd Engine Alarm

- D.38. Trim Gauges port/stbd
- D.39. Oil Gauges port/stbd
- D.40. Battery Gauges port/stbd
- D.42. Fuel Gauges port/stbd
- D.43. Engine Hours port/stbd
- D.44. Steering Wheel

- D.45. Trim Tabs
- D.46. Port/stbd Throttles Engine Tilt
- D.47. Kill Switch
- D.48. Antenna Selection Switch
- D.49. PRC 117 Headset

- D.50. Navigational Lights and Switches
- D.51. Aft/Forward Bilge Pump Switches
- D.52. Battery Gauges
- D.53. Main/Port/Stbd Battery Switches
- D.54. Emergency Switches
- D.55. Loud Hailer
- D.56. Engine Switches /Hour Meters

Compartment Lighting

There are 4-12 Volt DC red lights on the console for night vision preservation.

	Leaning Post
	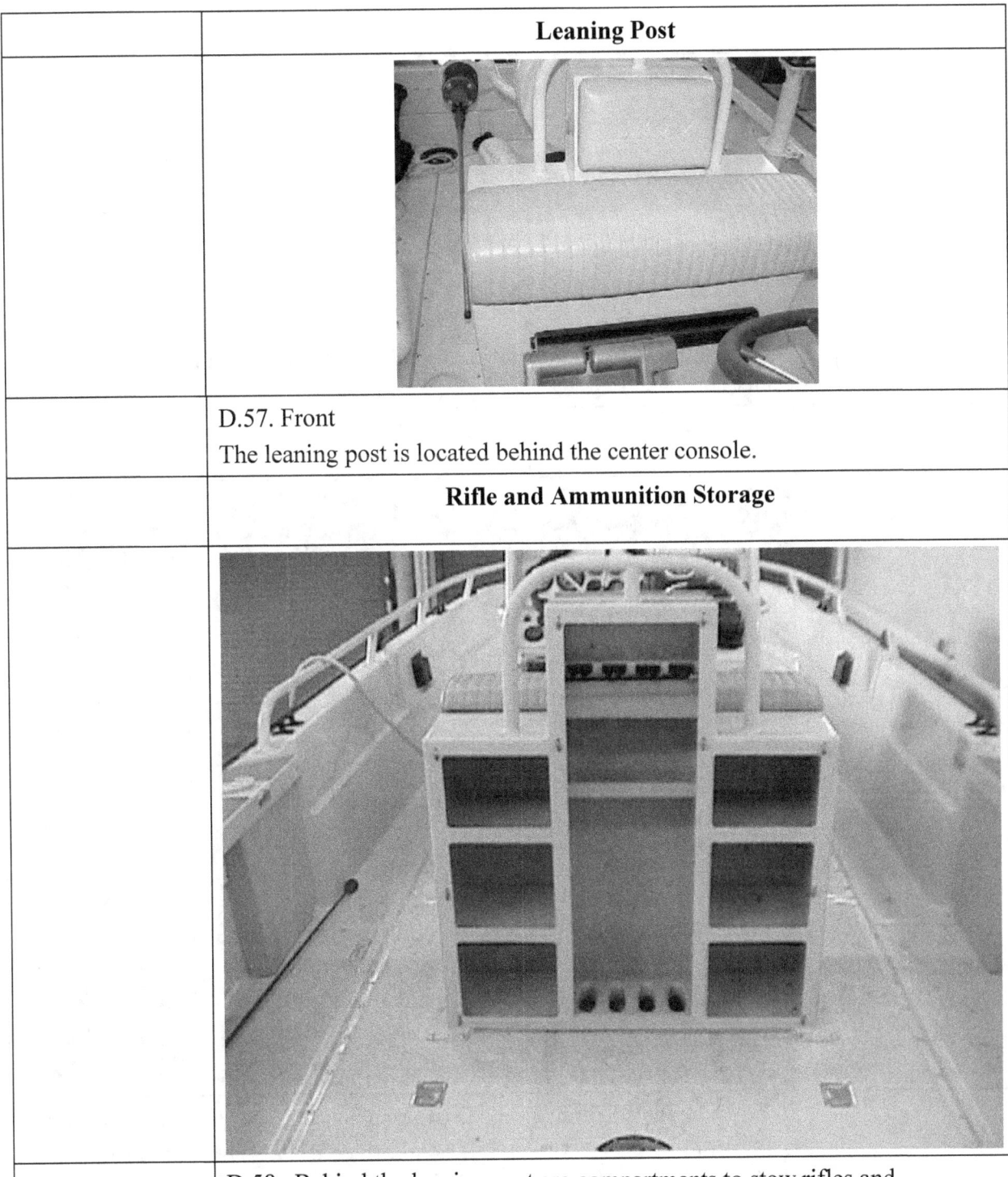
	D.57. Front The leaning post is located behind the center console.
	Rifle and Ammunition Storage
	D.58. Behind the leaning post are compartments to stow rifles and ammunition.

	Center Console Void
	D.59. The center console void is located between the leaning post and the center console.
	Aft
	D.60. Deck Plate Lifting Eyes D.61. Fuel Gauges D.62. Fuel Tank Void D.63. Void D.64. Port Void D.65. Stbd Bilge D.66. Drain Stoppers D.67. Fuel Gauge through hole plug

Port and Starboard M240B Gun Mounts

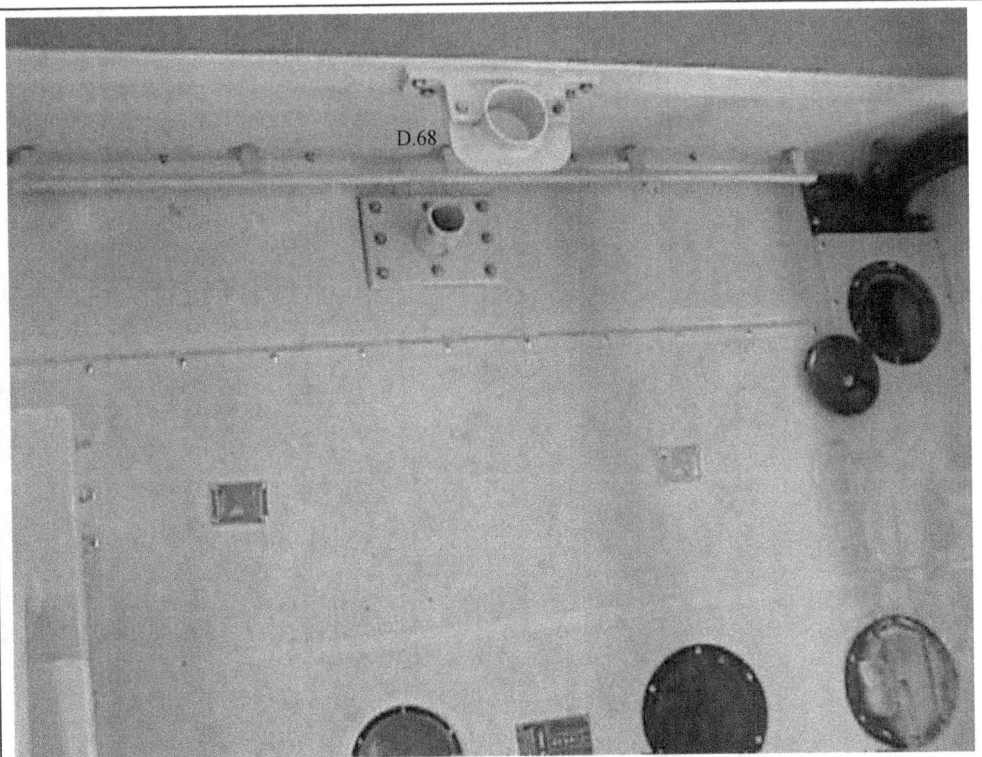

D.68. The TPSB has two M240B gun mounts. One mount is located on the starboard aft bulkhead and the second is located on the port aft bulkhead.

Stern
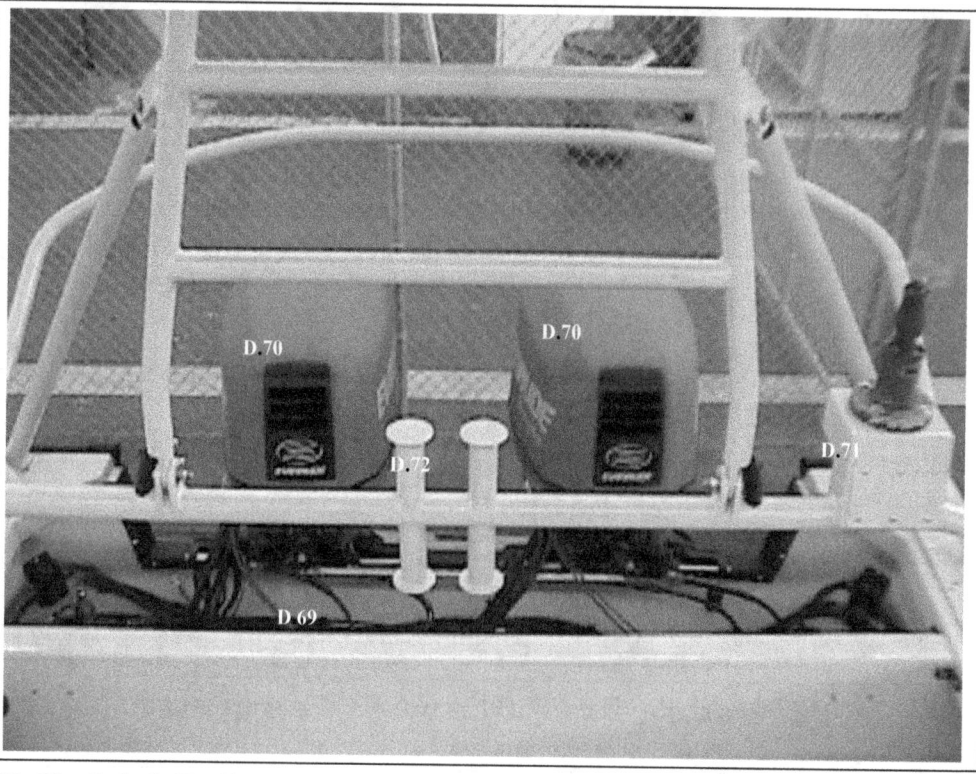
D.69. Splash Well   D.70. Port/Stbd Engines   D.71. PRC-117 Antenna   D.72. Tow Bitt   The splash well also contains the fuel/water separator; priming bulbs, VRO oil tanks and miscellaneous control lines, cables and steering rod arms.

Cage

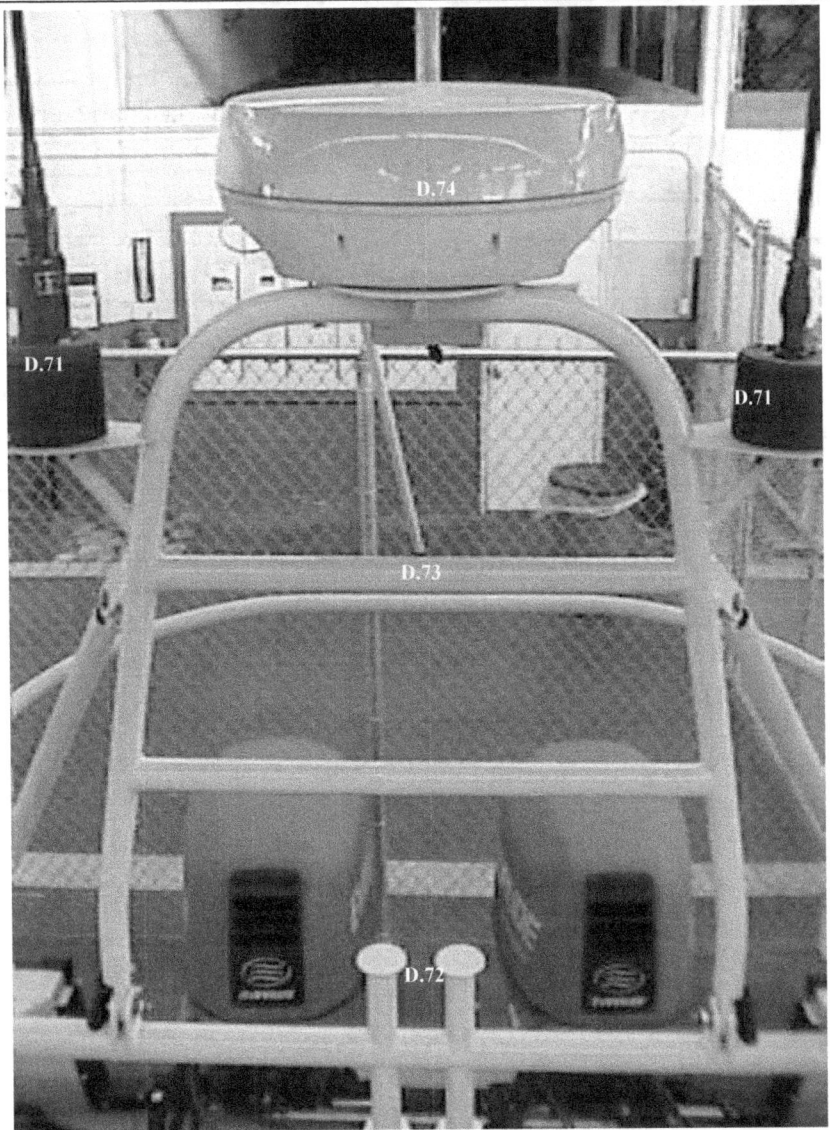

D. 71. PRC-117 Antennas   D. 72. Tow Bitt   D. 73. Cage   D. 74. Radar Dome Scanner

CHAPTER 3 BOAT SYSTEMS AND COMPONENTS

Overview	
Introduction	This chapter discusses the 25' TPSB's mechanical, electronic, and manual operating systems. It describes basic operating characteristics and provides information for efficient use of the equipment and for prevention of casualties.

In this chapter			
	Section	**Topic**	**See Page**
	A	Engine Oil System	3-3
	B	Fuel System	3-3
	C	Electrical System	3-5
	D	Engine Alarm System	3-9
	E	Steering System	3-11
	F	Fire Fighting Equipment	3-12
	G	Dewatering Equipment	3-12
	H	Lighting Systems and Siren/Loud Hailer	3-13
	I	Weapons Systems	3-15
	J	TPSB Outfitting	3-17

THIS PAGE LEFT INTENTIONALLY BLANK

Section A: Engine Oil System	
A.1. General	The Evinrude 175 FICHT engine oil system uses Bombardier TC-W3 outboard oil. Each of the two tanks holds 3 gals of oil. The oil system operates at a pressure of 6-20 psi and consists of 7 main components.
A.2. Tank	The tanks are located in the transom splashwell area. They are made of plastic with a removable cap for filling and a second cap that holds the oil level float and return fitting for the oil supply and return hoses.
A.3. Primer Bulb	The primer bulb is located in the transom splashwell area. It is inline with the supply hose to the engine and also acts as a check valve. Its function is to prime the oil system.
A.4. Oil pump	The oil pump is located on the fuel filter bracket, behind the air silencer. It is diaphragm-operated and driven by crank case pulses. It draws oil from the tank and supplies it to the oil injector. The oil pressure switch is mounted on the pump.
A.5. Oil Pressure	The oil pressure switch warns the coxswain and engineer if there is loss of oil pressure. It is normally closed and opens under pressure. The switch receives current from the Electronic Control Unit (ECU) and is activated if the pressure drops below 4+/- 1 psi. There is a programmed time delay that prevents false warnings generated by unusual boat operating conditions. The ECU will store a service code in memory, turn on the System Check "NO OIL" light, and the engine will go into Speed Limiting Operational Warning (S.L.O.W.) mode (will not come up in RPMs).
A.6. Oil Injector	The oil injector is an oil cooled 26volt solenoid similar in design and function to a fuel injector. It is located in front of the engine to the right of the fuel filter. It receives oil from the oil pump, and injects it at approximately 40 psi into the oil distribution manifold. The injector has an internal oil passage designed for cooling that never closes, and passes through the body to link the inlet and outlet nipples. The operation is variable and controlled by the ECU, and is relative to throttle position and engine rpm. The ECU can detect an injector open circuit and store a service code, turn on the System Check " NO OIL " light, and initiate S.L.O.W. A fuse in the Power Distribution Panel protects the oil injection circuit.
A.7. Oil Distribution Manifold	The distribution manifold receives oil under pressure from the oil injector. It has metered outlets and hoses, each of equal length.

Section B: Fuel System	
B.1. Tank	The fuel tank is a single 171-gallon welded aluminum tank and is permanently installed below the cockpit deck. The tank rests on a high-density rubber mat and is foamed into place. It is secured with aluminum straps. The tank is fitted with two ½" vent tubes, a 1-1/2"fill neck, a fuel level gauge and a fuel pick-up port. All the fuel tank fittings are located at the center of the tank. The fuel level indicator incorporates a tank-mounted gauge with an electric sending unit leading to the console-mounted fuel

	gauge. The tank mounted fuel gauge may be viewed through a 6" deck plate located at the aft end of the tank. An access plate in the deck allows access to two 90-degree elbows with aluminum pick-up tubes that extend to the bottom of the tank. The pick-up tube is removable for inspecting and cleaning.
B.2. Fuel Fill	A fuel fill pipe leads from the deck access plate to the center of the fuel tank. The fuel fill deck plate is clearly labeled "GAS". A standard two-point deck plate key is used to remove the threaded cap. The connection between the fuel fill hose and the fill neck on the tank may be accessed through an 8" plastic plate between the console and the leaning post.
B.3. Fuel Vent	The forward fuel tank vent tube is located adjacent to the fuel fill. The aft tank vent tube is located adjacent to the supply pick-up port. A 5/8" USCO Type-A hose connects the tank vent tube to the flush vent fitting. The vent tube is installed through the hull side just below the rubrail. The forward vent hose is routed with the fill hose and the vent fitting is located on the port side. The aft vent hose is routed with the supply lines and the aft vent fitting is located on the starboard hull side near the splash well. The flush vent fittings are screened and protected by small clamshell ventilators. An inverted loop formed from copper tubing is installed on the interior side of the flush vent fittings. The inverted loop helps to prevent seawater from entering the fuel tank.
B.4. Anti-Siphon Valve	An anti-siphon valve is located at the fuel tank, and keeps the system from back draining. It must be of sufficient size as to allow maximum fuel flow at all times.
B. 5. Fuel Supply	The fuel is supplied by a 3/8" ID USCO Type-A hose. The supply lines are routed from the pick-up port at the tank below the tank cover and over the starboard side. The supply hoses extend up through the grate over the bilge pump sump to the fuel water separator (OMC #174176) installed in the motor well for each supply line and each engine. Disposable fuel filter canister filter out dirt, lint, water and contaminants from the fuel. A fuel line with a primer bulb connects to each fuel filter that is connected to each fuel intake on the respective engines. The primer bulb is used to purge air from the fuel system and raise fuel line pressure in the engine prior to starting.
B.6. Fuel Filter	The canister type fuel filter is a water separator filter and is located behind the air silencer at the front of the engine. It is a 13-micron rated filter capable of filtering out objects larger than 13-microns. The fuel filter bracket provides a mounting point for the lift pump and the oiling system. The water sensor is located at the top of the fuel filter bracket, and receives current from the ECU. If water is present (approximately 3/8" above the bottom of the fuel filter canister), the sensor completes a circuit. This in turn switches on the **"CHECK ENGINE"** light and stores a service code in the ECU memory.
B.7. Lift Pump	The mechanical lift pump is a pressure-pulse type pump driven by crankcase pulses. It mounts piggyback on the rear of the fuel filter bracket at the front of the engine. The pump is operated by two pulse hoses and sends fuel directly into the filter through an internal bracket passage. Oil is received from the oil distribution manifold, and is mixed with the fuel prior

	to being sent to the fuel filter and prior to the vapor separator.
B.8. Vapor Separator	The vapor separator is located at the rear of the engine. It's serviced only as a fuel pump/vapor separator assembly. The vapor separator receives fuel from the fuel filter canister, then supplies fuel to the electric circulation pump for distribution to the fuel lines and fuel injectors. A water hose connects to the bottom of the vapor separator. Water flows upward to cool the fuel, and then exits the separator. The water cavity is self-draining when the engine is shut off. The fuel pressure regulator is internal and not serviceable. Return fuel from the injectors is routed to the base of the separator and through the fuel pressure regulator. The regulator maintains system pressure at approximately 20-30 PSI. A hose to a fitting in the port intake manifold connects the fuel vapor vent. Vapor pressure and low vacuum at the manifold combine to move vapor from the separator to the manifold. The vent's opening and closing is controlled by a float, needle and seat that are sensitive to fuel-height caused by the buildup of internal vapor pressure.
B.9. Fuel Injectors	The fuel injectors are 26-volt solenoids, and there is one per cylinder. The injectors are secured to the cylinder head by a flange and two 5/16". screws. Each injector has two ports; one for a fuel inlet, the other an outlet, both on the same side of the injector body. The inlets and outlets are different sizes to prevent fuel line mis-installation. Fuel injectors receive voltage from the Power Distribution Panel, which in turn receives it from the rectifier/regulator. A 10 amp mini-fuse protects one pair of injectors. Each injector has an internal fuel passage designed for cooling. It passes through the body to link the inlet and outlet nipples. Since fuel arrives under pressure, a small volume constantly flows through the injector to cool the coil and armature
B.10. Cooling System	The cooling system consists of a shaft driven impeller pump located in the lower unit of the outboard. It receives the water supply from the water pickup screens also located on the lower unit. The water is circulated through the power head then discharged through the prop.

	Section C: Electrical System
C.1. General	Primary power is derived from three (3) batteries. The batteries are 12Vdc wet cell sealed batteries rated at 105 ampere-hours/520 cold cranking amps. The batteries are located in the console and are stored in separate boxes. The battery boxes are nested in cut-outs through the console floor and are strapped to the deck. All three (3) batteries are charged automatically by the alternators on the engines through an isolator. Battery maintenance is important to assure that the boat will be ready for operation when required. Maintenance for the 105 amp wet cell battery is divided into the following four categories: 1. **Inspection**: Conduct a monthly inspection of the batteries to determine the following: • Terminals are secure and free of any visible signs of corrosion. • Coat the terminal ends with dielectric grease.

WARNING✋ **Batteries contain sulfuric acid, which is dangerous and can cause serious injury. Avoid contact with skin, eyes, and clothing. If contact occurs, flush the affected area with large quantities of water and call for emergency medical assistance.**	• Batteries are properly secured in the protective boxes, and the boxes have not been damaged. • Battery tray is securely fastened in place. • The battery does not show signs of cracking. 2. **Testing**: Battery voltage checks should be conducted on a regular basis. Checking the condition of the battery with a hydrometer should be done on a bi-weekly schedule. Should the hydrometer indicate that the battery is insufficiently charged, it can be charged by running the engine or by charging with the 4-bank battery charger. 3. **Cleaning**: At least once per year, or when the batteries appear to have dirt or corrosion on the terminals, they should be cleaned. To clean the battery, turn the battery switch to the "OFF" position. Disconnect the battery cables from the terminals. Remove the battery from the plastic battery box. Clean the terminals and casing with a solution of baking soda and water. Use a wire brush on the terminals. Keep the solution from entering into the cells. Wipe the battery and terminals dry with a clean dry cloth. Clean the battery cable ends in the same manner. Connect the cables to the appropriate terminals and recoat with dielectric grease. 4. **Charging**: The engine alternators charge the batteries when the engine is running. The batteries are charged through the Batt/Maxx unit, that allows up to three independent battery banks to be charged by two engines. The Batt/Maxx unit also prevents a higher charged battery from discharging into another lower charged battery by keeping the batteries electrically isolated from one another. If a battery fails to be charged by the engine battery, it might have to be replaced. Check the engine alternator for proper function according to the engine manufactures instructions and for loose wiring before replacing the battery.
C.2. Battery Switches	The three (3) batteries are connected to the +12 Vdc electrical system by rotary **"ON/OFF"** battery switches (Perko #9601). The engine starting battery switches are grouped together on the face of the console, near the port side. The outboard switch controls power to the port engine and is wired to the forward, port battery located in the console. The inboard switch, in turn, controls power to the starboard engine and is wired to the forward, starboard battery in the console. The electronics battery switch is also located on the aft face of the console, farthest to starboard. The electronics battery switch is separated from the engine start battery switches by the battery parallel switch. The electronics battery switch is wired to the aft most battery in the console. In order to start the engines, both engine start battery switches located on the outside of the console must be turned to the **"ON"** position.

NOTE	Never turn the battery switches to the "OFF" position when the engine is running. Serious damage to the engine's electrical system may result. When using the emergency battery parallel switch, release the switch once the engine has started or if engine starter is not cranking. The parallel system is designed for momentary use only and will be damaged if used continuously.
C.3. Port Engine Starting Battery Bank	The forward, port battery in the console services the port engine (ignition, gauges and starter) and the ship's service loads. The port engine starting battery bank is controlled by the port battery switch on the aft face of the console. The power feed from the port battery switch leads to a fuse panel mounted to the front of the console. The fuse panel is protected by a black plastic cover. The fuse panel provides direct power and over current protection to the console interior light and to the hand-held spot light. A positive jumper cable connects the fuse panel to the commercial switch panel through a distribution buss. The commercial switch panels includes individual toggle-breakers that control power to the navigation lights, depth sounder, strobe light and instrument back lighting. Power is also supplied to the auxiliary switch panel that contains six (6) additional spare toggle breakers. A 50 amp push-to-reset breaker is included in the feed cable between the battery switch and the fuse panel to proved over-current protection for the circuit. The breaker is located inside the aft, starboard corner of the console
C.4. Starboard Engine Battery	The forward, starboard battery in the console provides power to the starboard engine ignition, gauges, starter and the electric bilge pumps. The starboard engine starting battery bank is controlled by the starboard battery switch on the aft face of the console. The port and starboard engine starting batteries may be momentarily connected in parallel by a 750 amp solenoid installed adjacent to the battery switches. The parallel solenoid is activated by a momentary switch on the console, located adjacent to the engine start battery switches. The bilge pumps are wired directly to the starboard engine starting battery through the dual bilge pump control panel. In-line fuses protect the bilge pump circuit.
C.5. Electronics Battery Bank Auxiliary	The aft most battery in the console serves the electronics and communication equipment. The electronics battery bank is controlled by the battery switch on the aft face of the console, farthest to port. The electronics battery switch is wired to the electronics distribution panel mounted to the inside of the fire extinguisher recess. A single conductor connects the battery switch to the main 50-amp breaker that will control power to the communications equipment. The remaining breakers on the electronic distribution panel control power to the VHF radio, the Raytheon radar and the loud hailer. A diagram of this bank can be found in Appendix B.
C.6. Maintenance	The DC electrical system requires little maintenance by the crew. Periodic Checks should be made to determine that all electrical connections are tight and free of corrosion, that no wires have been damaged, and that the protective cover is in place over the bus bar.

CAUTION!	Inspect wiring inside of console for signs of damage caused by storing equipment in the console or corrosion on a regular schedule. If connection has become loose due to vibration or if a wire needs to be replaced, turn off the battery switches prior to performing any maintenance. It is recommended that all electrical connections be coated with liquid neoprene or other appropriate corrosion inhibitors.
C.7. Flywheel	The FFI flywheel has four important functions: • Provides a ring gear for starter motor engagement. • Has cast-in timing encoder ribs on the outer diameter that work in conjunction with the magnetic crankshaft position sensor to control ignition timing and fuel injector operation. • Acts as a fan to cool the stator and ECU. • Magnets that work in conjunction with the stator to provide power to operate the ignition, injectors, ECU, and boat accessories
C. 8. Stator	The stator, in conjunction with the flywheel and rectifier regulator, makes up the FFI system alternator. It consists of two 3-phase windings that produce AC voltage. Stator output is directed to the rectifier/regulator.
C.9. Rectifier/ Regulator	The rectifier/regulator is located underneath the ECU. It receives AC current from the alternator, rectifies/regulates 12 and 26-volt outputs, then supplies it to the Power Distribution Panel. It sits in a water-cooled pocket on top of the block. The rectifier/regulator has a number of specialized features: • An inductor that acts as a current (amperage) limiter to help protect the fuel injectors • An isolator to allow installation of an auxiliary battery without needing to purchase an after market battery isolator • A voltage suppresser to protect the entire 12-volt electrical system from damaging voltage
C.10. Starter Solenoid	The starter solenoid is similar in operation to those found on other outboard engines. It's located near the top of the power head midway along the starboard side. Its only function is to engage the starter motor.
C.11. Main Power Relay	The main power relay is located at the starboard rear of the powerhead. It supplies switched 12V power to the Power Distribution Panel, and maintains the circuit necessary to charge the battery.
C.12. Power Distribution Panel	The Power Distribution Panel is located on the upper starboard side of the powerhead. It receives battery 12V power from the solenoid, 26V power from the rectifier/regulator, and switched 12V power from the main power relay. It's responsible for the operation and protection of virtually all FFI engine circuits. It mounts four 40 amp relays and seven automotive type mini-fuses. The cover is sealed to prevent water damage, and stores a small fuse removal tool. A wiring diagram can be found in Appendix B.

Section D: Engine Alarm System

D.1. S.L.O.W. Warning System	FFI engines have a protective feature that prevents powerhead damage due to an engine cooling system overheating, loss of oil pressure, alternator output exceeding 26 volts, or excessive ECU temperature. This feature is called **S**peed **L**imiting **O**perational **W**arning (**SLOW**). A number of devices monitor engine-operating conditions. All are linked directly to the ECU, which in turn is connected to the dash-mounted System Check gauge and horn. **Initiation**: When the appropriate sensor or switch is activated, the ECU responds by interrupting fuel injector operation. It begins a gradual three to five second drop in engine RPM to a threshold limit of approximately 1800 RPM. This is accomplished by cutting out one cylinder at a time, until a total of three are affected. The ECU simultaneously sounds a dash-mounted warning horn and turns on the appropriate **System Check** gauge light. As long as SLOW is activated, the engine will run normally below 1800 RPM. Above 1800 RPM, the engine will run poorly. **Recovery**: The engine will operate as described as long as the condition that activated SLOW continues to exist. To recover from SLOW, two conditions must be satisfied: • Sensor or switch parameters must be back within limits; • And engine RPM must be reduced to idle. The system will now immediately recover and the ECU will return engine operation to normal.
D.2. Electronic Control Unit (ECU)	The Electronic Control Unit (ECU) is located at the top rear of the powerhead. It has two 24-pin engine harness connectors. It is a water-cooled microprocessor that receives sensor, switch, and electrical signals that provide information on engine operating conditions. All provide data to help the ECU control engine operating parameters such as spark advance, fuel flow, and oiling. The ECU also sends electrical commands to various powerhead components to control engine operation. When a failure is detected, a service code is stored in the ECU that maintenance personnel may access to remedy the problem(s).
D.3. Internal ECU Sensors	Five sensors are located inside the ECU: • Barometric pressure • ECU temperature • Alternator 26 volts • Battery 12 volts and • ROM verification. Since none are serviceable parts, failure correction would require replacement of the ECU.
D.4. Barometric Pressure (BP)	The Barometric Pressure (BP) Sensor is a silicon pressure sensor having a diaphragm- sealed air passage that generates an AC voltage signal. It senses ambient air pressure through a screened port that's open to the atmosphere.

	The BP signal enables the ECU to compensate for changes in sensor altitude and air density up to 14,000 f. (4267 m) so it can adjust fuel flow accordingly
D.5. ECU Temperature Sensor	The ECU Temperature Sensor monitors fuel injector driver circuitry temperature to prevent it exceeding design limits. One or more fuel injectors would malfunction should this occur. The ECU will also initiate *S.L.O.W.,* but only if excessive temperature is the failure mode.
D.6. RPM Limiter	The RPM Limiter is a feature of ECU programming that prevents engine damage due to excessive RPM. At 6200 RPM, fuel and ignition to even numbered cylinders are shut off. At 6500 RPM, fuel and ignition to the remaining cylinders are also shut off. Normal engine operation automatically returns as soon as engine RPM drops down to the specified range.
D.7. Idle Governor	The Idle Governor reacts to water temperature sensor values. It changes fuel pulse width to maintain engine RPM within a rage of 650 RPM (warm engine) to 850 RPM (cold engine), The governor is inactive above 1000 RPM.
D.8. Volt Circuit Sensor	The 12-Volt Circuit Sensor monitors rectifier/regulator 12-volt output. This is the circuit that supplies all 12-volt component/circuit requirements? If voltage is out of limits, high or low, the ECU will store a service code and turn on the "**CHECK ENGINE**" light.
D.9. ROM Verification	The ROM Verification is a continual ECU self-test of factory programming. The ECU will turn on the "**CHECK ENGINE**" light and store a service code if, at any time, a program failure is detected.
D.10. Air Temperature Sensor	The air temperature sensor monitors the temperature of air entering the air silencer. The AT sensor is a Positive Temperature Coefficient (PTC) thermistor, a resistor whose resistance changes with temperature and alters voltage values accordingly. When temperature increases, both resistance and voltage also increase. When temperature decreases, resistance and voltage likewise decrease.
D.11. Water Temp Switch	FFI engines have a Water Temperature Switch located in the starboard cylinder head. It threads into a seat in the water passage of the head, but does not actually contact water. It monitors water temperature to protect against an engine overheat. Its operation differs somewhat from the water temperature sensor in that it's an on/off switch, not a thermistor.
D.12. Water Temperature Sensor	The Water Temperature Sensor is located in the port cylinder head. It threads into a seat in the water passage of the head, but does not actually contact the water. The sensor has a dual purpose; it provides data to the ECU primarily for use in adjusting the air/fuel ration during engine warm-up, and it will trigger the **System Check** warning gauge during an engine overheat.
D.13. Shift Interrupt Switch	The Shift Interrupt Switch is in contact with the shift lever. The switch is normally open; when the button is depressed (by excessive shift loads), the switch is closed and completes a ground circuit. The ECU then shuts off fuel and spark to three cylinders (No. 2, 4, and 6) for six revolutions

	(approximately 3 seconds) to momentarily reduce drive train loads and ease shifting, then automatically restores normal engine operation. The signal threshold is 2500 RPM; the shift interrupt function will not work above it. The switch must be released to its normally open position before the interrupt circuit can be acuatated again.
D.14. Throttle Position Sensor	The Throttle Position (TP) Sensor is a rotary potentiometer. It's located near the flywheel cover, and contacts the top of the vertical throttle shaft. The sensor receives a voltage signal from the ECU. As the throttle lever is rotated, the ECU receives a return voltage signal through a second wire. This signal is relative to the position of the throttle shaft. As the throttle opens, voltage increases. As the throttle closes, voltage decreases. A third wire completes the ground circuit back to the ECU.
D.15. Crankshaft Position Sensor	The Crankshaft Position Sensor is a magnetic device. It generates a magnetic field that's interrupted by the flywheel encoder ribs passing through it. This produces an AC voltage signal directly related to flywheel RPM. Crankshaft TDC is determined by encoder rib spacing. The sensor feeds the flywheel encoder data to the ECU, which calculates crank position and engine speed. The ECU generates a tachometer signal, and controls fuel injector and ignition operation. The sensor is located on the port side of the flywheel cover just in front of the starter motor, and requires a 0.050 ± 0.005 in. (1.27 ± 0.127 mm) sensor-to-flywheel air gap to operate properly.

Section E: Steering System

E.1. General	When the steering wheel is turned to starboard (clockwise), hydraulic oil is pumped out of the helm unit, into the starboard hydraulic line and then into the cylinders. As the oil is pumped into one side of the steering cylinder, an equal volume of oil is displace out of the opposite side pushing the cylinder rod to port. The cylinder rod is attached directly to the engine which rotates the engine counter-clockwise and puts the boat into a starboard turn. Turning the steering wheel in the opposite direction results in a similar system response but in an opposite direction. When no course corrections are required, the integral lock valve holds the engine in place.
E.2. Steering Wheel	The steering wheel is a 16" non-magnetic stainless steel Attwood wheel. It is located on the port side of the center console.
E.3. Helm Pump	The Seastar II Helm Pump is an axial piston pump specifically designed for manual steering. It has a built-in lock valve to prevent the steering load from feeding back to the helmsman. The lock valve will not allow the outboard to move unless the steering wheel is turned. The oil is displaced out of the cylinder flows back to the helm unit.
E.4. Hydraulic Ram	The Hydraulic Ram is a piston-type connected to the front of the outboard via mounting plate adapters.
E.5. Tie Bar	The tie bar is an adjustable stainless rod that connects the two outboards so that they are mechanically connected and act as one.

Section F: Fire Fighting Equipment	
F.1. Fire Extinguisher	The TPSB is equipped with one (1) 5lb, Type 1, dry chemical fire extinguisher. Pulling the pin and squeezing the handle activates the unit. The fire extinguisher is located in a recessed open compartment on the outboard, port side of the center console.
WARNING ✍	**A dry chemical extinguisher does not cool or remove oxygen from fire tetrahedron. It is effective in only knocking down the flames. If enough heat or ignition source is present, the fire will reflash after powder settles from the air. Class A chemical extinguishers are LEAST effective on Alfa fires.**
F.2. Collapsible Pail	The TPSB has one (1) vinyl nylon reinforced collapsible pail. The pail has a two (2) gallon capacity. It is carried on the shelf under the coxswain stand.

Section G: Dewatering Equipment	
G.1. Bilge Pump	The TPSB has two (2) 12-volt DC submersible type bilge pumps. One is located in the anchor locker directly under the center console, amidships. This pump has a 500 gph (gallons per hour) capacity and discharges through a hull fitting on the starboard side. The aft bilge pump is located under the deck cover on the starboard side, in front of the false transom. This pump has a 1000 gph capacity and discharges through a deck fitting on the starboard side a few inches above the water line and athwart the pump. A third bilge pump will be found on older hulls (darker gel-coat). This pump is located on the port side aft, just in front of the false transom. This pump has a 1000 gph capacity, and discharges through the port side hull fitting, athwartships from the pump.
G.2. Scuppers	The false transom has two (2) scuppers to assist deck drainage. The scupper is a "through" fitting with a rubber flap that allows water to flow one way from fore to aft. This allows water to flow into a transom well shelf under the coxswain stand.
G.3. Drains/Drain Plugs	There are two "through" hull drains on the TPSB. The forward drain is located in the forward void below the .50 cal gun mount on the aft starboard side corner. The aft drain is located to the outboard side of the bilge pump, forward of the false transom on the starboard side. Both drain plugs are rubber expansion type with a brass T-handle tightening system. Always inspect boat before launching. Ensure plugs are installed correctly. Periodically, inspect plugs to ensure their condition. Although the TPSB will not sink if the plugs are missing, the water intrusion will cause extra drag, electrical failure, instability on the hull, and excessive wear on the bilge pumps. **Always ensure plugs are tightly installed before launching.**

Section H: Lighting Systems and Siren/Loud Hailer

H. 1. Operation NOTE	The navigational light toggle switches are located on the console switch panel. The running lights are controlled with the switch labeled "**Nav Light**". **The masthead light may be controlled separately by the switch labeled "Anchor Light".**
H.2. Mast and Running Light	The red and green running lights are mounted forward, atop the gunwhale panels, on the port and starboard sides. The masthead light is located atop the flag mast on the tow bar tower. **Side** **Lens Color** **Degree of Arc** Port Red 112.5 degrees Starboard Green 112.5 degrees Masthead White 360 degrees Anchor White 360 degrees
H.3. Spot Light	The hand held spotlight is located just inside the port access on the center console. The light is a 300,000-candle power light. It's waterproof and protected in a rubber housing.
H.4. Deck Lights	The deck lighting system is a series of four (4) red colored light fixtures located under the gunwhales from amidships to stern on both the port and starboard sides. When illuminated they cast a red light on the deck and lower interior gunwhales that does not illuminate the structures above the gunwhales while at the same time preserving the crew's night vision.
H. 5. Blue Strobe Light	The forward blue law enforcement strobe light and siren are incorporated in single cast aluminum housing, mounted atop the forward side of the console, port side of the boat centerline. The high intensity dual halogen light is controlled by a toggle switch marked "**strobe**" on the main console switch panel. The aft blue LE strobe is mounted just below the radar stand, atop the tow bar tower. The same switch that operates the forward strobe also operates the blue LE strobe and aft strobe light.
H.6. Siren/Loud Hailer	The siren / loud hailer is located on the front side of the console. See G.16. The control panel for these devices are flush mounted on the control console, near the starboard side just below the radios. The "**on/off**" switches for the siren / loud hailer, tow selector switch, siren, horn, P/A volume control, and microphone jack are located on the control panel. The amplifier is mounted on the inside of the console in a waterproof enclosure.
H.7. Comms	The radio is a Motorola Spectra Marine Transceiver. The radio covers a VHF FM frequency range of 156.050 to 157.425 MHz. The radio has a built in voice-scrambling feature. It is located just below the radar display enclosure in its own enclosure. The radio is equipped with a VHF 150 watt marine antenna that is mounted atop the tow bar tower, just behind the radar mount.
H. 8. Radio	The TPSB carries the AN/PRC 117 transceiver. The transceiver has VHF, UHF, HF, and SINCGARS (Single Channel Ground and Airborne Radio

System-DOD) interoperability. In addition, the radio has modem capabilities to the functions of the AN/PRC-117D hopping radio and has integrated COMSEC capability that is compatible with the Vinson KY-57/58 equipment. The transceiver has eight channels. The manual channel is used for selecting programming parameter such as frequency, bandwidth, channel mode, and changes to the transmit power control when used in low power. Channels 1-7 are preprogrammed.

Frequency Range	**Bandwidth**	**Modes**	**Channel Spacing**
30.000-89.975	WB only	FM only	25
116.000-173.995	WB only	AM or FM	5 or 6.25
225.000-419.995	WB or NB	AM or FM	5

Wideband   (WB) – 30KHZ
Narrowband (NB) – 15KHZ

The transceiver is mounted on top of the console in an aluminum box and is easily slipped in or out. It can be locked down with 2 side retainers. The system has three antennas mounted at different positions on the tow bar tower. A selector for these antennas is located on the lower dash next to the handhold on the starboard side.

H.9. **Radar** **NOTE**	The TPSB is equipped with the Raytheon Pathfinder SL-70 Radar. It has a LCD (Liquid Crystal Display). The radar display is mounted inside a weatherproof enclosure on the starboard side of the console dash. The enclosure slopes forward and drains through a weep hole in the forward port of the console. A clear panel covers the display and has removable hinges to access the display. A toggle breaker inside the console near the port access door controls power to this unit. The radar scanner is mounted atop the tow bar tower. Range setting: FM 1/8 NM to 24NM. **Consult the specific SL-70 Radar Manual to become familiar with all functions, proper setup, and operations of this unit.** The SL-70 radar can interface with the Raytheon 398 GPS/LORAN unit for full function radar/DGPS information display. Operating guidelines can be found in Appendix C of this manual.
H.10. Global Positioning System (GPS)	The TPSB is equipped with the Raytheon 398 GPS / loran unit. The GPS display is mounted on top of the console dash, affixed to a metal bracket mount. Power to this unit in controlled by a breaker inside a console, near the port access door. The GPS receiving antenna is located just forward of the compass repeater, atop the console dash, just aft of the spray shield.
H.11. Compass	The TPSB is equipped with the Richie MC – 200B compass with remote sensor. The electric compass card is located atop the console dash, forward of the GPS, and next to the PRC-117D box. The electronic compass sensor is located in the forward of the anchor locker, and is attached to the underside

	of the deck. The sensor is protected with a plastic box cover. The locker is accessible through the watertight flush aluminum deck hatch, just forward of the console. The unit has one (1) power button, one (1) light button, and a reset detent button under the compass card. **Operating guidelines can be found in Appendix C.**
H.12. Depth Finder	The TPSB carries the Raytheon L 750 Depth sounder. The unit has a LCD display and is a multi-functional, monitoring depth, speed, water temp, and underwater targets. (i.e. Fish). Toggle breakers on the main console switch panel control the power. The display unit is mounted directly above the helm and just above the engine gauge on the face of the center console. The transducer for the unit is mounted externally on the transom centerline, between both engines and below the waterline.

Section I: Weapons Systems

I.1. Machine Gun .50 Caliber Browning M2 Heavy Barrel	The TPSB is equipped with (1) .50 cal M2 Heavy Barrel. This weapon can be used effectively against personnel, light armored vehicles, low/slow flying aircraft, and small waterborne craft. The weapon is a belt fed, recoil operated, air-cooled, crew-served machine gun. The gun is capable of firing single shot and automatic. **Data:** Weight 84lbs Length 64 inches Fed Link Belt Operation Recoil Muzzle Velocity 3050 feet per second (fps) Max Range 6800 meters Max Effective Range 1830 meters Cyclic Rate of Fire 450-550 rounds per minute (rds/m) The .50 cal M2 HB is mounted on the forward gun mount pedestal (MK16 MOD 8) and is secured to a soft mount (MK 93 MOD). At the base of the gun mount pedestal are two (2) trays to hold extra .50 cal ammunition boxes.
WARNING	**Improper headspace and timing can cause malfunctions, damage to the gun, and injury to personnel.**
I. 2. Machine Gun M240B	The TPSB, when fully manned, should carry two (2) M240B machine guns. The M240B is a general-purpose weapon capable of being fired from several mounts or hand held. It is effective against personnel, slow/low flying aircraft, and small, unarmored watercraft. The M240B machine gun is an air cooled, link belt fed, gas operated, crew served weapon. The operating cycle begins from an OPEN bolt position. The weapon features a fixed headspace, which permits rapid barrel change-outs. **Data**

	Weight 27.6lbs Length 49 inches Feed Link Belt Operation Recoil Muzzle Velocity 2800 feet per second (fps) Max Range 3725 meters Max Effective Range 1810 meters Cyclic Rate of Fire 600-650 rounds per minute (rds/m) The mounts for the M240B are located on the port and starboard side, just behind the coxswain bench. The M240B is mounted to the gun mount pedestal (MK 16 MOD 8) and is secured to the cradle mount (MK 97 MOD 0). Extra ammunition storage is located inside the coxswain bench on the shelving, accessible from the rear of that stand.
WARNING ☝	**The bolt fires from the open position. Always ensure weapon is on safe and clear when not in use.**
I.3. Rifles M16A2	The M16A2 is a lightweight, magazine fed, gas operated, shoulder fired weapon. The rifle can be stored behind the coxswain bench in mounts specially fitted for that purpose. The max effective range for the A2 is 800 meters and the max range is 3600 meters. The A2 fires semi-automatic and bursts of three (3) rounds.
I.4. M203 Grenade Launcher	The M203 grenade launcher is designed for use with the M16A2 rifle. The M203 fires a 40mm grenade, and must be reloaded with every shot (single shot).
I.5. Pistol, M9	The M9 9mm pistol is carried by the coxswain. It is a semi automatic, magazine fed, recoil operated, double action weapon. The M9 has a fifteen (15) round capacity. The max effective range is 50 meters.
I.6. M870 Remington 12-Guage Shot Gun	The M870 is a manually operated, magazine (tube) fed, pump action, shoulder or hip fired weapon. This weapon can also be stored in the weapons compartment behind the leaning post. The M870 is effective in boardings and alongside interrogations. The M870 12-gauge Coast Guard Tactical has been specifically designed to fire a variety of lethal and non-lethal 12-gauge ammunition, greatly expanding its operational capabilities. Lethal 12-gauge ammunition includes "00" buckshot, with a maximum range of 40 yards, and a lead slug, with a maximum effective range of 75 yards. Non-lethal 12-gauge ammunition included "sting-ball" rubber buckshot, with an effective range of 5-15 yards. All non-lethal, or less than lethal, 12-gauge ammunition must be used in accordance with the Maritime Law Enforcement Manual, COMDTINST M16247.1 (series) and Ordnance Manual, COMDTINST M8000.2 (series). When non-lethal ammunition is loaded into the M870, a bright yellow "stock sock" must be installed around the shoulder stock.

Section J: TPSB Outfitting

J.1. Anchors	The TPSB carries a 14lb. Danforth, galvanized spool anchor. Attached to the anchor is a 3/8" shackle, and 5 feet of chain. The anchor is secured on mounts, located just forward of the central console. The anchor line is approximately 150' 3-strand nylon, 1 ¼" in circumference. It is located in a plastic box behind the leaning post. This line can be used as a towing line if necessary.
J. 2. Lines and Mooring **NOTE**	The TPSB carries a minimum of 4 lines. Those lines are usually 5/8", 3-strand nylon in lengths of 25' and 15'. **Three (3) strand is easier to splice and maintain in the field than DBN (Double Braided Nylon).**
J.3. Paddles and boat hooks	The TPSB had two (2) paddles and one aluminum boat hook. This equipment is secured with straps to the inner gunwales, next to the port and starboard gun mounts.
J.4. Fenders	Four (4) 8"x30", gray (or black) fenders are used aboard the TPSB. Fenders Should have approximately 10 feet of line spliced to them. The fenders are made fast to the tow bar.
J.5. Survival Equipment	The TPSB carries one (1) 20" ring buoy. The life ring is usually hung over the two bitts for easy access during operations. The throwable survival heaving line is found on the shelf behind the leaning post. The TPSB is fitted with a first aid kit, which is stowed on the upper shelf behind the leaning post.
J.6. Pyrotechnics	The TPSB carries pyrotechnics other than that carried in the crew survival vest. This pyro serves as supplementary survival equipment, but is also used in tactical port security operations as illumination devices. The MK 127 parachute flare is a launchable parachute with a white phosphorous burning flare. The TPSB carries six of this type. One (1) MK 79 flare kit is carried aboard the TPSB. This does not include those carried in the survival vests. The MK 124, day/night marker is also carried on board the TPSB. Quantities of twelve (12) are issued to the TPSB's. This does not include the ones carried in the survival vests. The MK 79s, 124s, and 127s are carried in sealed containers. They are stowed on the lower shelf of the coxswain bench near the weapons storage.
J.7. Ammunition	The TPSB provides several spaces and compartments for ammunition storage. Boxed ammo can storage shelves are located behind the coxswain bench. Ammo can storage racks are located under the .50 cal gun mount, and the anchor locker and gunwale, the tie down bars and the four (4) aft and two (2) forward flush deck pad eyes can be utilized to tie down ammo cans and extra barrels.
J.8. Flags	Two flags are normally flown from the small mast atop the tow bar tower. The national ensign is hooked to, and flown higher than the Coast Guard ensign.
J.9. Canopy	The TPSB comes equipped with its own canopy assembly. Better known as The "Conestoga cover", the canopy covers the main deck from just before the center console forward to the false transom astern. The frame for the

	canopy consists of three (3) aluminum tube "ribs", which are mounted athwartships, in separately adapted female fittings attached to the gunwales. With the stanchion in place the canvas is secured to the stainless steel rope, and for and aft stanchions with three (3) strand nylon line. The entire unit is held in place with four (4) wire guys with turnbuckle tensioning devices. The two (2) guys astern fit onto eyes at the tow bar base and the two (2) forward guys attached to stainless steel eyes on each railing forward.
WARNING ✋	**Each canopy should be checked for proper fit and missing or damaged parts. The canopy is adjusted for the hull that it was manufactured for, resulting in differences from boat to boat.**
J.10. Air Horn	The handled air-horn aerosol can type air-horn is stowed behind the leaning post in one of the built-in shelves.
J.11. Navigation Kit	One (1) navigation kit in a watertight bag containing various charts of AOR, stopwatch, nautical slide rule, pencil, parallel plotter, dividers, speed wheel, and one handed magnetic compass for back up, in-case the electrical compass fails. This is stowed inside the center console or radar box for easy access to the coxswain.

CHAPTER 4 THE CREW

Overview

Introduction	The 25' TPSB is designed and configured to support PSUs as an inshore/harbor surface interdiction response asset in accordance with Required Operational Capabilities (ROC) and Projected Operational Environment (POE) for Coast Guard Port Security Units (PSU), COMDTINST 3501.49 (series). The Coast Guard places great trust in the abilities of its boat crews to perform the sorties and missions assigned to them. The professional seamanship skills and knowledge required of a crew to safely and efficiently complete an assigned PSU mission can only be developed and maintained through successful completion of required training, diligent study of platform, weather and mission characteristics, and consistent practice of essential skills in the required operational environment. Members of an assigned crew must develop confidence-building skills under relatively safe conditions before using these skills under maximum hostile conditions. The Coast Guard has provided minimum standards and guidelines for building skills, which are part of the certification process required by the Boat Operations and Training Manual Volume I and II, COMDTINST M16114.32 (series) and COMDTINST M16114.33 (series). The general duties of the crew are described in this chapter.

In this chapter

	Section	Topic	See Page
	A	Crew Size	4-3
	B	Boat Crew	4-3

THIS PAGE LEFT INTENTIONALLY BLANK

Section A: Crew Size

A.1. General	The minimum crew for a 25' TPSB engaged in OCONUS port security operations is three: one coxswain, one engineer, and one crewmember. A PS member may be added when operational requirements exist. Due to the small size of the crew, cross training in the duties of other positions is essential. Additional members may be required during special operations. Where local staffing permits, additional crewmembers will first ride in a training capacity to increase their proficiency with the boat's equipment and operation. Minimum crew requirements for other situations can be found in the Boat Operators and Training Manual Volume I, COMDTINST M16114.32 (series).

Section B: Boat Crew

B.1. Coxswain	The coxswain is in charge of the boat and its crew during all sorties and missions. TPSB coxswains must maintain currency and certification requirements in accordance with the Boat Operations and Training Manual Volume I and II, COMDTINST M16114.32 (series) and COMDTINST M16114.33 (series). The coxswain represents the Commanding Officer or Officer-in-Charge, and has authority and responsibility independent of rank or seniority. Coxswains must be familiar with United States Coast Guard Regulations, 1992, COMDTINST M5000.3 (series), and the Boat Crew Seamanship Manual, COMDTINST M16114.5 (series), which outlines this relationship. In addition, Coxswains must be familiar with all PSU policies and procedures. Completion of TPSB Coxswain Level 1 Module 2.3 through 2.3.19 and TPSB Tactics Level II Coxswain Module 2.4 through 2.4.32 is required. The coxswain is responsible, in order of precedence, for: • Safety and conduct of passengers and crew • Safe operation and navigation of the boat • Completion of the sortie or mission(s) • Safeguarding of life and property • Compliance with Federal laws and regulations. • Compliance with the Rules of Engagement (ROE) • Conducting boat check-off's
B.2. Engineer	TPSB engineers must maintain currency and certification requirements in accordance with the Boat Operations and Training Manual Volume I and II, COMDTINST M16114.32 (series) and COMDTINST M16114.33 (series) for both engineer and crewman. Some of the engineers responsibilities may include:

	• Engines and all power equipment • Assisting in boat navigation, line handling, lookout, towing watch, or helmsman • Radio operation • Make minor underway repairs • Gunnery
B.3. Port Security Member	The port security member is responsible for: • Assisting the crewmember in securing the boat's equipment and line handling • Lookout • Manning 50 caliber machine gun when required
B.4. Crew Member	TPSB crewmen must maintain currency and certification requirements in accordance with the Boat Operations and Training Manual Volume I and II, COMDTINST M16114.32 (series) and COMDTINST M16114.33 (series). The crewmembers responsibilities include: • Securing the boat's equipment • Line handling • Serving as a lookout, anchor watch, firefighter, swimmer, or helmsman • Radio operation • Gunnery

CHAPTER 5 BOAT OPERATIONS

Overview	
Introduction	Boat handling is a complex skill that requires extensive knowledge and practical underway experience to build confidence and skill levels.
NOTE	**The Boat Crew Seamanship Manual, COMDTINST M16114.5 (series) and Boat Operations and Training Manual Volume I and II, COMDTINST M16114.32 (series) and COMDTINST M16114.33 (series), provides a large amount of information on boat handling. Coxswains shall be very familiar with these instructions before operating the TPSB.**
In this chapter	

THIS PAGE LEFT INTENTIONALLY BLANK

Section A: Starting Procedures

A.1. Pre-start	Before starting a cold engine and before each mission, carry out the following steps:	
	Step	**Procedure**
	1	Be sure all bilges are free of unsecured equipment or materials (e.g., loose rags, tools, or cleaning gear).
	2	Be sure all bilges are free of fuel, oil, and water and boat plugs are in.
	3	Energize the battery switches to the "All" position and the Main breaker panel located under the console.
	4	Check Fuel level and Variable Ration Oiler (VRO) tank levels.
	5	Ensure the throttles are in the neutral position.
	6	Push in engine plungers switches, hour meter and FICHT engine check system should commence.
	7	Depress the starter button and hold until engine starts. If engine will not start within 15 seconds let it stand for 30 seconds and repeat the procedure. Do **NOT** squeeze fuel bulbs or advance throttles if engine does not start.
	8	When engine starts, check for raw water discharge; which will be a straight stream from outboard discharge hole.

Section B: Underway Operations

B.1. NavBrief	All crewmembers will receive a navigation brief by the coxswain before getting underway IAW Coast Guard Navigation Standards Manual, COMDTINST M3530.2 (series). Safety, engineering and navigational status, emergency procedures, weather and operational risk management considerations will be discussed. Procedures for operational risk management are outlined in Operational Risk Management, COMDTINST 3500.3 (series).
B.2. Pre-Underway Checkoff	Prior to getting underway, the TPSB Underway Check-off list shall be completed. A copy of this list can be found in Appendix E. **1. Prior to launching, the following items should be checked:** • Docking drain plugs located adjacent to each of the two (2) aft electric bilge pumps are installed • Fire Extinguisher, floatation devices and signaling equipment in proper working condition and stowed. • Battery condition. • Anchor, anchor line and mooring lines on board and properly stowed. • Spare parts and tool kit onboard and stowed properly. • Fuel and oil levels are adequate. • Bilge pumps are functioning properly.

	<ul><li>Navigation lights operate properly.</li></ul>**2. Prior to starting engines:**<ul><li>Turn all battery switches located on the console on the "**ON**" position.</li><li>Squeeze fuel primer bulb and oil injection bulb until hard.</li><li>Place engine shift lever in neutral position.</li><li>Lower engine and trim all the way "**IN**" (down).</li><li>Inspect surrounding water and area adjacent to boat for possible hazards</li><li>The push to start panel breakers are engaged.</li></ul>**3. After starting the engine:**<ul><li>Return throttle to idle.</li><li>Visually verify cooling water flowing from engine.</li><li>Verify that engine is running properly (No excessive/abnormal noise and/or vibrations).</li><li>Check voltmeters.</li><li>Observe external fuel lines for leaks. Check steering operation.</li></ul>
B.3. Gauges	After getting underway, closely observe the steering console gauges. They indicate system-operating conditions. Gauge readings should be within following ranges:<table><tr><th>Gauge</th><th>Idle</th><th>Cruising</th></tr><tr><td>Tachometer</td><td>650 RPM in Gear</td><td>4000 RPM</td></tr><tr><td>Water Temperature</td><td>140-185 degrees F</td><td>140- 185 degrees F</td></tr></table>
B.4. Corrective Action	During boat operations, if change occurs in any of the systems (e.g., abnormal gauge readings, vibration, or unusual handling characteristics), take corrective action to prevent further damage.
B.5. Throttles	The 25' TPSB responds quickly to the throttles. Increase speed gradually to allow engines to warm-up thoroughly. Unless absolutely mission essential, avoid rapid increases in speed when main engines are cold.

Section C: Maneuverability

C.1. General	With its powerful twin 175 FICHT outboards, the TPSB is a highly maneuverable boat. An experienced coxswain can steer, turn, and dock this boat with ease. However, this boat is designed with a deep V for larger seas and higher speeds in relatively choppy waters (1-3ft). It also has a low transom for the outboards. These features, desirable for fair weather, can easily become highly undesirable characteristics in foul weather. Safe operation requires the following actions:

	Step	Procedure
	1	Take into account the boats limiting factors.
	2	Continuously monitor the prevailing weather and sea conditions.
	3	Know the boat and its positive handling features, as well as the crew's limitations.
C.2. Outboard Engine RPMs		The maximum safe operating RPM for this boat is 5,700 (approximately 46 knots). However, during normal operations never use more than 90 percent of the engines' maximum safe operating RPMs. This 90 percent figure equates to a normal engine-operating limit of 5,100 RPMs (approximately 41 knots). The 10 percent extra power and speed is the boat's main defense in most threatening situations.
C.3. Limitations		The following chart gives the upper limits which should be observed when operating in the given sea states. The upper limits shall not be exceeded. In addition, the shape and period of the seas may sometimes require even slower speeds to avoid hull damage.
		Seas (ft) **Engine RPMs** **Speed in Knots** 0-2 4000-5700 30-46 2-4 2500-4000 20-30 4-6 1000-2500 05-20
NOTE		**TPSBs are fully mission capable when operating in less than 2' seas and 30 knot winds. TPSBs can operate in up to 6' seas for short periods.**

Section D: Head Seas

D.1. Operating in Head Seas	Traveling into head seas normally presents no problems if operations remain within the defined wind and sea limiting factors.
D.2. Maximum Steering Control	To maintain maximum steering control, keep the outboards as deep in the water as possible.
D.3. Crew and Armament Protection	To protect the crew and armament in head seas, apply ample power just before passing through the crest of the wave. This will cause the bow to lift and prevent head seas from breaking fully onto the deck.
WARNING	**The TPSB is not designed to operate in breaking seas, surf, or "white water". TPSB coxswains are reminded not to operate in these dangerous areas.**

Section E: Dead in the Water

E.1. Operating in Calm Conditions	During calm weather and sea conditions, any wind will cause the 25' TPSB to lay with its stern into the wind and the bow away from the wind. This is due to the boat's center console and its shallow draft forward. To maintain positive control, maintain minimum steerageway. The pivot point of the 25' TPSB is at its aft section of the center console.
WARNING ☝	TPSB (fully loaded condition) can swamp when dead in the water if hit astern by a 6-foot breaking wave. Capsizing could occur in larger than 6' sea conditions. It could be instantaneous with little time to react. TPSBs are not to operate in surf conditions.

Section F: Capsize Prevention

F.1. Statistics	As of 2003, one 25' TPSB has capsized with no loss of life. This occurred while operating in a large wake from a vessel. Excessive speed and bad judgment were leading factors to the mishap.
F.2. Assess The Situation	If a life-threatening situation does not exist, departure from the safe operating limits may create one. Use good judgment and proper risk assessment if called on to exceed those limits. Consider whether lives are clearly in danger and whether the 25' TPSB is the best resource available. Departing from the established operational limits will severely test the coxswain and crew. Boat crew survival may quickly replace mission performance as the primary concern.
F.3. Operate Within Limitations	If the operating limits are exceeded, the boat will be in a "danger zone." The chances of capsizing are greatest while operating in the danger zone. Near shore, conditions frequently occur which could easily place a boat in the danger zone.
WARNING ☝	**Strictly observe the operating limitations of the 25' TPSB. Avoid breaking waves or surf. Remain with the boat if it capsizes. The Design of the 25' TPSB will remain afloat for some time if capsized. Remain with the boat to stay afloat; keep the crew together to aid search and rescue.**
F.4. Capsizing Conditions	The force needed to capsize the 25' TPSB is most likely to come from heavy following seas or large breaking waves striking on the beam. Some of the listed conditions which could contribute to a capsizing: <ul><li>Breaking waves 6 feet or higher;</li><li>Tidal current ebbing or the boat proceeding against a strong tidal current with steep, following seas;</li><li>Reduced stability due to low fuel level, excessive water in bilges, or</li></ul>

	topside icing.
	• Excessive personnel or equipment on board
	• Large wake from a vessel and excessive speed
F.5. Corrective Action	If any of the above conditions occur, take positive control and execute immediate corrective action to maximize and maintain boat-handling capability. Remember the full power maneuver at the last minute to lift the bow to prevent a full wave break onto the deck. If the boat takes a sea over the stern, filling the deck, use extreme caution when maneuvering to come about. If the deck is flooded, the boat will be sluggish and may not respond well when coming about. **Always be aware of changes in the wind, waves and currents!**
NOTE	**Always observe the service requirements for wearing hypothermia protective clothing, personal flotation devices, and boat crew signal kits.**

Section G: Towing

G.1. General	The 25' TPSB was designed for fast, immediate response. This hampers the effective towing capacity of the TPSB. Nonetheless, good seamanship and general knowledge of small boat handling and towing is required. Towing should not be rendered to other disabled vessels except in the case of an emergency or under instruction from the OTC (Officer in Tactical Command). Towing procedures as set forth in the Boat Crew Seamanship Manual shall be followed.
G.2. Line Handling	Towing procedures shall be followed as per the Boat Crew Seamanship Manual, COMDTINST M16114.5 (series) and Boat Operations and Training Manual Volume I, COMDTINST M16114.32 (series). As a reminder, this vessel may encounter situations where it has to tow another TPSB during times of increased stress or operational tempo where it puts both crews at great risk. Line handling and rigging of tows should be done at a bare minimum. **This is a must and can't be over-emphasized.**
WARNING	**Line handling during stressful situations can be very dangerous. If there is a line around the towing bitt the aft gunners on the towing TPSB shall have a means of removing the towline from the vessel as rapidly as possible. If the situation dictates, both TPSB's will be manning their weapons while still maintaining a means of towline removal. When adjusting the towline, the crewmember must increase the distance between their hands and the towing bitt to prevent their hands from being pulled into the bitt. Jewelry shall never be worn when handling lines.**

G.3. Combat Towing	During combat operations, a TPSB may require towing due to combat damage or mechanical failure. The OTC will assess the situation and may direct another TPSB to render aid to the disabled boat. The threat level will dictate how the boat is towed.

Section H: Man Overboard

H.1. General	It is the responsibility of the coxswain and each crewmember to know where their fellow crewmembers are. In the instance of a crewmember over the side, the reporting crewmember acts as observer, maintaining sight on the lost crewmember and point so as to guide the coxswain back to the scene. In the case of the coxswain being lost over board, the lanyard to the kill switches will stop the engines, requiring a back-up lanyard to restart the engines and return to the scene. **DUE TO THE HIGH MANUEVERABILITY OF THE TPSB, MAN OVERBOARD DRILLS MUST BE PRACTICED REGULARLY.**
H.2. Action	Upon notification, the crewman throws a fender, or type IV life ring, over the side and yells, "**Man overboard port/starboard/astern side**". The coxswain then activates the GPS, maneuvers the boats, sounds the danger signal, and notifies the OTC. As quickly as is possible, the boat is brought back to the missing crewmember. Putting a swimmer in the water to assist the individual is not recommended as often the boat operates with only three qualified crewmembers. To lift a conscious individual back aboard, two people are required. Once the individual has been recovered, appropriate first aid should be administered. If on a patrol, the coxswain must request, from the OTC, permission to return to base.
H.3. Non-Crewmember	During military operations, if the Person In the Water (PIW) is not a crewmember (did not fall off the TPSB), the coxswain **MUST** evaluate the PIW as hostile. Flotation devices may be thrown to assist the individual, but under no condition should any attempt be made at recovery. The coxswain should notify the OTC immediately. In a non-deployment, training situation, the reporting TPSB will treat the PIW as a SAR situation and recover them as soon as possible. Immediate notification should be made to the unit with radio guard and to the nearest CG SAR facility.

Section I: Firefighting

I.1. General	Fire fighting equipment on a TPSB is limited. The TPSB is not equipped with firefighting personal protective equipment (PPE) or adequate firefight gear to combat a fire on another vessel. The fire extinguisher is intended for use on the TPSB and not for assisting another boat. As in all cases, after reporting to the OTC, the coxswain may be directed to assist another vessel in distress, but in doing so, the patrol sector will be left unguarded. The

	TPSB should be relieved prior to departing his sector, unless otherwise directed by the OTC. In a non-deployed status, the coxswain reports the fire on another boat to the nearest Coast Guard SAR facility. The TPSB then remains on scene to render assistance until such a time that they are relieved by the SAR facility or another Coast Guard SAR asset.
I.2. Operation	In case of fire: • For open oil or fuel spill fires, discharge the dry chemical fire extinguisher in a sweeping motion across the base of the flames. • For compartment fires, discharge should be directed into the fire at the base of the flames. • For running, dripping fires from leaks in fuel lines or tanks, start extinguishing at the lower part of the fire and work upward. • Shut off or otherwise stop the leak if possible. • In the case of an electrical fire, secure the electrical system by turning off the main battery switches located on the console. After the electrical system is secured, extinguish the fire.
I.3. Maintenance	The needle on the fire extinguisher pressure gauge should remain in the green zone. Check for broken seal or signs of white powder on the discharge nozzle. If either is observed, replace the unit. All damage control equipment shall be maintained and recorded IAW USCG Damage Control Technical Publication 2006 (series).

Section J: Damage Control	
J.1. General	The Boston Whaler is designed to remain afloat even when the hull has been penetrated. After reporting the situation, all attempts should be made to stem the flow of water, or to secure equipment that has become damaged (i.e. engine, mast, gun mount, etc). Members should ensure that PFDs and Distress Signal Kits are donned. Notify the OTC immediately.

Section K: Anchoring	
K.1. General	Under normal operating conditions, the TPSB will not be anchored while on patrol as mobility is its number one form of defense. Under special conditions, anchoring may be necessary. Suitable anchorages shall be part of the mission/navigation brief. The OTC will direct the coxswain where the maneuver is to be accomplished. While in a non-deployed status, the coxswain is to anchor out of the channel, utilizing all available navigational tools to determine a suitable location.

K.2. Action	The coxswain will direct a crewmember to break out the anchor and inspect all connections and lines. Upon command, the anchor will be lowered over the TPSB's bow. Slow backing down on the engines will produce sternway to assist in setting the anchor. The coxswain will determine how much anchor line is to be paid out, depending on the type of bottom, sea conditions and depth of water. Once the anchor is set, a fix will be taken to ensure that the anchor is holding.
K.3. Recovery **NOTE**~	The crewmember recovering the anchor will report to the coxswain when the anchor line tends up and down. Upon command from the coxswain, the anchor will be lifted free of the bottom and brought back on-board. After cleaning, the anchor and anchor line will be returned to the anchor locker-plastic box in the leaning post seen in Chapter 2 section J-1. **During anchor evolutions, it is imperative that crewmembers maintain constant communications with the coxswain.**

Section L: Ice Operations

L.1. Ice Limitations	The 25' TPSB is **NOT** to be operated in ICE or SLUSHY conditions. The ICE and SLUSHY conditions will prevent the outboards from sufficiently recirculating water through the impellers. The resulting hull stress will shorten the life of the boat even if the hull is not penetrated.

Section M: Tactical Operations

M.1. Introduction	Port Security Units (PSUs) provide force protection in critical OCONUS port areas during military contingencies. The PSU will conduct routine inner harbor patrols; provide moving and stationary security zones; enforce moving and fixed security zones; and provide waterside security around critical facilities or vessels.
M.2. Boat Tactics	PSU 25' TPSB boat tactics are defensive in nature and adaptable to different operational and threat environments. Waterside security measures and boat tactics are prescribed in Volume VII – Port Security – Marine Safety Manual, COMDTINST M16000.12 (Chapter 7), and are currently included in the resident training curriculum delivered by SMTC.

Section N: Securing Procedures

N.1. Procedures	Upon mooring after a mission, take the following steps, in the given order, to secure the boat properly and to prepare it for the next mission:	
	Step	**Procedure**
	1	If recently run at high RPMs, allow the engines to idle 2 to 3 minutes for cool-down.
	2	Secure all electrical and electronic equipment.

	3	Shut down Engines using the engine stops, secure all electronics
CAUTION!	**4**	Trim outboard engines in the "UP" position. Depress the engine hour plungers and Secure the Battery switches. **Engine plungers must be depressed or engine hour meter will continue running if Main Battery switches are left on.**
	5	Secure Main 12 volt breaker panel.
	6	Switch bilge pumps to "AUTO".
	7	Top off Fuel Level and VRO tanks.
	8	Conduct visual inspection of propeller.
	9	Stow all Gear on boat.
	10	Wash down boat with fresh water.
	11	Complete underway Abstract of Operations. Report and discrepancies to the Engineering Officer. **The mission is NOT complete until the boat is ready for the next mission.**

CHAPTER 6 MISSION PERFORMANCE	
Overview	
Introduction	The performance procedures in this chapter are specifically designed for Transportable Port Security Boats. These boats are Standard Coast Guard boats designed specifically for military operations. The TPSBs purpose is to provide waterside security to critical infrastructure and high value vessels moored within ports and harbors, and provide escorts for high value assets entering and leaving the port and harbor or transiting the area of operations assigned to the PSU. The TPSBs are fully mission capable when operating in less than 2 foot seas and 30 knot winds, if necessary, the boats can operate with a degraded mission capability in up to 6-foot seas for short periods. TPSB's are not designed or authorized to operate in surf conditions. The TPSB's can interdict lightly armed, (small arms, shoulder fired rockets, etc) and lightly armored vessels less than 100 feet in length. TPSB's can also be used to interdict subsurface infiltrators using standard anti-swimmer procedures. Normally, three TPSBs are used to provide a layered point defense to the assigned assets. This layered defense works with both stationary and moving assets.

In this chapter	Section	Topic	See Page
	A	Launching, Trailering, Lifting/Sling	6-3
	B	Mission Briefing	6-3
	C	Outfitting	6-4
	D	Patrol	6-4
	E	Weapons and Pyrotechnics	6-5
	F	Safety	6-5
	G	Medical	6-5

THIS PAGE LEFT INTENTIONALLY BLANK

Section A: Launching, Trailering, Lifting/Sling	
A.1. General	TPSBs can be launched in either of two ways: • A trailered boat may be backed into the water using a designated launch ramp. • A suitable crane can lift a TPSB from its trailer and set it in the water.
A.2. Key issues	Before backing the TPSB into the water or lifting, ensure all drain plugs are in and trailer tie downs removed. When launching from a trailer, the radar mast and engines should be in the raised position, with the engine locks in the up/off position. When lifting by either using the lift points or slings, the radar mast and engines must be in the down position.
WARNING ✋	**Exercise extreme caution when lifting boats. The entire lift crew must wear hard hats and be trained in lift operations. All personnel involved in lifting operations must be thoroughly familiar with Coast Guard policy and procedures as well as applicable guidance from the base or facility at which the lifting is taking place. Unit command officers will ensure that adequate safety measures are adhered to during all lifting operations. The crane operation and all personnel involved in the lifting operation will be taking commands from the designated lift captain and a safety officer shall be observing.**

Section B: Mission Briefing	
B.1. General	The OTC will outline the entire defensive plan, and the assigned task that the TPSB will perform during the patrol. Secondary tasks will be explained as well as operational conditions, communication plans, call signs, situation update and passing of intelligence.
B.2. Preparation	The coxswain will supervise the preparation of the TPSB for the mission. The crew will perform assigned check-offs (Appendix E) and provision the TPSB with all necessary stores: Food, water, fuel, oil, ammunition, medical supplies and any additional required equipment. A complete equipment load-out list for the TPSB is included in Appendix D.

NOTE✍	Prior to leaving the dock/mooring to get underway, the crew will verify that all communication, navigational, weapons and engineering systems are functioning properly.

Section C: Outfitting

C.1. General	As directed during the mission brief, the crew will load the TPSB with equipment and provisions per TPSB standards. Small arms, in small arms locker, ammunition in designated ammunition bins, water and medical stores in correct bins.
WARNING✋	No materials/tools will be stored inside console as damage may be inflicted on electrical equipment.

Section D: Patrol

D.1. Execution	The TPSB coxswain will conduct all patrols in designated areas as specified by applicable patrol orders and other guidance from the Officer in Tactical Command (OTC) as well as Coast Guard and Theatre Commander requirements. Radio contact will be maintained with the OTC and other TPSB's in the patrol area IAW the published communication plans and special tasks will be accomplished as directed by the appropriate higher authority. Clear communications between the coxswain and crew are vital especially when maneuvering (ie coming right or coming left) and making speed changes. Operating the TPSB within operating limitations is absolutely essential to crew and boat safety.
D.2. Harbor Checks	At any time, your TPSB may be directed to scout a particular area within the security zone, and make reports as required.
D.3. Transfer Personnel	At any time, your TPSB may be directed to pick up and transport an individual or item from one location to another.
WARNING✋	Extreme care must be taken when approaching piers and other boats/ships. Underwater objects, cables, and rocks may await you below the surface. Swift tides, winds, and waves may affect maneuverability. Crewmembers will be working on deck, slow operations and alertness is in order.
D.4. Sonar Buoys	Your TPSB may be required to place sonar buoys. At your pre-brief you should be instructed where and when this operation is to be done. You may be given instructions on how to activate the buoy or an individual may be added to your crew to deploy the device(s).
WARNING✋	This operation requires working over the side. All crewmembers must be alert to activities on the boat as well as in the operating area. PFDs and required survival equipment shall be worn IAW Coast Guard Regulations.

Section E: Weapons and Pyrotechnics

E.1. General	The TPSB is outfitted with a single .50 Cal forward firing crew served machine gun and two M240B side mounted crew served machine guns. In addition, as dictated by local command, MK3A2 concussion grenades may be carried for anti-swimmer operations.
NOTE	**When weapons are aboard the TPSB, it shall be guarded by at least two personnel armed with personal defense weapons.**
	Personally assigned long weapons are stored in the aft weapons locker, usually two M16 automatic rifles and an M870 riot shotgun are on-board. Ammunition for the machine guns is stored in the aft storage bins as dictated by the unit arming order, or under the forward mount. Pyrotechnics are stored in the designated aft storage bin.
E.2. Maintenance	At each shift change, all weapons are checked for operation and cleanliness. Salt spray is wiped off and exterior metal parts lubricated. At least, once each day, all crew served weapons shall be completely dissembled and thoroughly cleaned and lubricated. Unit operating policy will designate when this is done.

Section F: Safety

F.1. Personal Protective Equipment	The TPSB is a highly maneuverable, fast boat. It accelerates and loses speed quickly, and is responsive to wave action (bounces). In a boat that can literally turn circles in a little over it's own length at high speeds, centrifugal forces can actually throw crewmembers over the side. All personnel embarked in the 25' TPSB shall be outfitted in accordance with the Rescue and Survival Systems Manual, COMDTINST M10470.10 (series).

Section G: Medical

G.1. General	Each TPSB is equipped with a Coast Guard approved medical kit, suitable for treating minor injuries.
G.2. Action	In the case of a medical emergency, render basic first aid and notify your Officer in Tactical Command (OTC) immediately.
G.3. Resourcefulness	Because of the limitations of available medical equipment, you may need to improvise, i.e. Meals Ready to Eat (MRE) bag could be used to cover a sucking chest wound. A paddle or boat hook tied in place with a mooring line could be a splint. A M240B ammo pouch could be used as a sling or tourniquet, etc.

CHAPTER 7 EMERGENCY PROCEDURES AND CASUALTY CONTROL

Overview

Introduction	This chapter describes emergency procedures and actions to be taken if a casualty to the boat or one of the boat's systems occurs. The best casualty control action is to prevent casualties through good maintenance and proper seamanship. If a casualty does occur, there must be timely execution of a predetermined plan of action to correct and/or prevent worsening of the situation. Frequent underway casualty control drills both prepare and improve the crew's response.
Casualty Control	Casualty control is the positive action taken to correct, control, and/or combat operational discrepancies experienced during underway operations. Due to the nature of Coast Guard missions, corrective casualty control measures can affect a range of operational situations from the potential loss of life to minor hull or machinery damage.
In this section	

Section	Topic	See Page
A	Fire	7-3
B	Runaway Engine	7-4
C	High Water Temperature	7-4
D	Collision with a Submerged Object/Running Aground	7-5
E	Loss of Steering	7-5
F	Engines Fail to Start	7-6
G	TPSB Disabling Casualties	7-6

THIS PAGE LEFT INTENTIONALLY BLANK

Section A: Fire	
A.1. General	This type of casualty presents a common threat to operations. The most logical and best preventative action is to remain alert and take early corrective action when fire-threatening conditions are observed. Evaluate every fire or potential fire and take corrective action.
A.2. Engine fire	The most likely location of fire on the 25' TPSB is the engine. Therefore, a physical inspection of this equipment is critical. Prior to getting underway remove the engine cover and inspect the hoses and wiring for any cracking or chafing.
WARNING ✋	**The fumes from an engine fire can be toxic. Ensure all personnel on board are aware of this and keep away from any smoke or fumes emitted from the engine.** If an engine fire occurs when the engine cover is off secure the engine and use the portable sodium bicarbonate dry chemical fire extinguisher to put out the fire. If a fire erupts when the engine cover is on, secure the engine and the battery for that engine. Secure the air vents by stuffing them with rags, shirts, mooring lines or any other materials available. Crimp the fuel supply line to the effected engine. If you do not have the means to crimp the line **DO NOT** cut it. Use the collapsible pail to pour water on the engine cover to help remove the heat from the fire. Call for assistance and return to base using the remaining engine (if possible). **DO NOT** attempt to remove the engine cover while underway. Removing the cover will supply the fire with oxygen and increase the risk of having a crewmember fall overboard while attempting to remove the cover.
A.3. Other Fires	Proper use of fire extinguishers can quickly extinguish small Class B and Class C fires. If an electrical fire occurs, first secure the appropriate breaker(s) to the affected piece of equipment. If necessary, secure the main breaker

Section B: Runaway Engine

B.1. Procedure	If there is a main engine runaway casualty during normal operation, immediately take the following corrective actions:	
	Step	**Procedure**
	1	Try to reduce the affected main engine's RPM by bringing both engines back to the "clutch engaged" position, keeping a load on the affected engine.
	2	If the main engine continues to runaway, press the engine stop button (kill switch) for the affected engine.

Section C: High Water Temperature

C.1. Procedure	If main engine jacket water coolant reaches 205°F, it will activate the alarm (buzzer) system and energize a red indicator light (located below the affected engine tachometer). If this occurs, immediately take the following corrective actions:	
	Step	**Procedure**
	1	Reduce RPM's to clutch ahead on both engines.
	2	Identify affected engine.
	3	Notify crew and OTC of casualty.
	4	Check overboard discharge.
	5	If temperature continues to rise secure the affected engine.
	6	Raise the engine out of the water and check for any debris that may be blocking the raw water intake ports.
	7	If necessary, rig the anchor.
	8	Notify OTC of situation.
	9	Return to base if damage cannot be repaired underway. If on patrol, remain until properly relieved or directed by OTC.

Section D: Collision With a Submerged Object/Running Aground

D.1. Procedure		If the boat strikes an object in the water or runs aground, immediately take the following corrective actions:
	Step	**Procedure**
	1	Reduce RPM's to neutral on both engines.
	2	Notify crew and OTC of casualty.
	3	<u>Coxswain</u>: Verify position.
	4	Trim engines out of the water and check lower unit and props for damage
	5	Engage engines at various speeds to check for vibration.
	6	Notify station of situation.
	7	Inspect hull at next haul out.

Section E: Loss of Steering

E.1. Signs	If there is a loss of steering control while underway, bring the boat to dead in the water (at most, maintain bare steerageway). Then investigate to determine the cause. Likely causes of steering loss include: • broken tiller bar / hydraulic ram, • broken hydraulic hose(s), • jammed engine, or • helm or helm pump failure. If the helm turns freely without any effect on the engines, suspect a broken hydraulic hose, air in the system, or leaking fitting. If the helm will not turn, suspect a jammed engine or hydraulic ram. Avoid backing on either shaft until the cause of the steering loss is determined and the proper actions are taken.
E.2. Steering Hose Broken	To regain control if a hydraulic hose is broken, follow these steps.

	Step	**Procedure**
	1	Bring both main engine throttle controls to the neutral or minimum steerage clutch position if in a running sea. Try to put the seas on the bow.
	2	Notify crew of casualty.
	3	<u>Coxswain</u>: Steer with engines, if needed.
	4	<u>Engineer</u>: Investigate the casualty.

	5	Crewman: If necessary, rig the anchor.
	6	Notify OTC of casualty
	7	If casualty cannot be repaired, anchor and call for assistance.
E.3. Jammed Engine	To regain control with a jammed rudder, follow these steps.	

	Step	Procedure
	1	Reduce RPM's on both engines. Bring both main engine throttle controls to the neutral or minimum steerage clutch position if in a running sea. Try to put the seas on the bow.
	2	Notify crew and OTC of casualty.
	3	Coxswain: Steer with engines, if needed.
	4	Engineer: Investigate the casualty.
	5	Crewman: If necessary, rig the anchor.
	6	Trim the engines out of the water and look for any debris that may be preventing the engines from pivoting on the trim plate.
	7	If causality cannot be repaired, notify base and return to base by steering with the engines throttles or await assistance.

Section F: Engines Fail to Start

F.1. General	If the main engines will not turn over when the starter button is depressed check that the battery switch is in the "on" position and the throttle is in neutral. If the engine will turn over but will not start check the following; • Ensure the kill switch lanyard is properly connected. • Check the fuel level • Ensure the fuel line is primed. • Ensure that the fuel lines are not crimped or pinched.

Section G: TPSB Disabling Casualties

G.1. General	If a disabling casualty is identified, the boat shall not get underway until the discrepancy is corrected. In the event the boat sustains a disabling casualty while underway, the boat shall immediately return to the nearest safe mooring. In some cases the boat may require assistance from another TPSB. If the disabling casualty takes place while conducting tactical operations, the OTC shall be notified and a decision will be made based upon operational necessity. The following is a list of Disabling Casualties: • Loss of Fathometer

	• Loss of Compass • Loss of radar capability in visibility less than 1 nautical mile • Engine Casualty • Radio Casualty/Loss of Communications

Appendix A 25' TPSB ENGINEERING CHANGES	
Overview	
Introduction	The two approved Engineering Changes (previously known as Boat Alts) for TPSBs directs the addition of the CRP-NAV 398 GPS Display and the CRP-RAYSTAR 112LP Compact GPS Sensor to be installed onboard of all of the 25' PSU boats. The second directs the upgrade of the VHF-FM antenna mount.

THIS PAGE LEFT INTENTIONALLY BLANK

DEPARTMENT OF TRANSPORTATION U.S. COAST GUARD 278 (Rev. 6-98)	BOAT ALTERATION	BOATALT NO. 25PSU-A-01 DATE JUN 29 1999

From: Commandant, U.S. Coast Guard (G-SEN)

To: Commanders, MLCPAC(v), MLCLANT(v)

Copy To: CG PACAREA, CG LANTAREA, UTB SYS CTR, CG YARD, CG ELC, CG NMLB School, G-OCS
CG ELC(014) (016) (024) (027) G-OPD PSU (305) (307) (308) (309) (311) (313) (TRADET)

Title: 25 PSU GPS Installation	BoatAlt Class: A [X] B [ ] C [ ]

Haulout required: [ ] YES [X] NO	Applies to the following boats: CG PSU 25341 (77) thru CG PSU 25384

Weight: 5 (lbs) [X] Added [ ] Removed K.G. CHANGE +/- 00.0 (ft)	Compensation Required: (Explanation enclosed) [ ] YES [X] NO

Description:

1. Purpose: This class "A" BoatAlt directs the addition of the CRP-NAV 398 GPS Display and the CRP-RAYSTAR 112LP Compact GPS Sensor to be installed onboard all of the 25'PSU boats. Completion of this BoatAlt will ensure standardization in the PSU fleet.

R. J. Formisano

R. J. FORMISANO

By Direction

DATE COMPLETED	ACTUAL COST $ _____ MAN HOURS _____ BOAT NUMBER(S) _____

INSTRUCTIONS: A copy is sent by the MLC to the operating unit to be kept in the boat record until the BOATALT is completed. Upon completion of the BOATALT, the unit is to forward a completed and signed copy to the Group and retain a completed and signed copy in the boat record. Groups to forward in accordance with MLC SOP's.

BOAT NUMBER AND UNIT	OFFICER IN CHARGE OR COMMANDING OFFICER

PREVIOUS EDITION IS OBSOLETE

2.   **BACKGROUND**: This system, which consists of the RAYSTAR 112LP Compact GPS Sensor and the NAV398 GPS Display assembly, has been installed on the last eleven 25'PSU boats being built by Boston Whaler. The first 33 boats were built without this system being installed. This BoatAlt will authorize the installation of this system on the remaining 33 PSU boats to keep the PSU fleet standard.

3.   **REFERENCES:**

3.1   <u>REFERENCES ALREADY PROMULGATED</u>: None

3.2   <u>REFERENCES PROVIDED BY SEPARATE CORRESPONDENCE</u>:

    (a) CG Plan Maintenance System 42315/015 rev 1
    (b) CRP-NAV 398/GPS/Loran Operations Manual

3.3   REFERENCES ENCLOSED:

    (c) Enclosure (1) Manufacturer's Drawing CB-9007,8,9 sheet 3 of 13

4.   **MATERIALS REQUIRED:**

    (1) CRP-NAV 398 GPS Display and mounting brackets.
    (2) CRP-RAYSTAR 112LP Compact GPS Sensor and mounting brackets

5.   **EQUIPMENT REMOVAL**: None.

6.   **EQUIPMENT INSTALLATION:**

6.1   Place the RAYSTAR 112LP GPS sensor brackets 16.25 inches from the right edge of the center console opposite of the steering wheel, behind the compass as shown in figure 1 and enclosure 1. Mark the bracket position holes using the mounting brackets as a template. Drill holes to accept four ¼ inch 10/24 stainless 316 marine grade bolts. Drill a hole (½ inch in diameter) 1-inch centered behind the mounting bracket to accept the GPS sensor cable. Mount the RAYSTAR GPS sensor bracket to the top of the console using ¼ inch marine grade lock nuts and bolts. Route sensors cable through ½ inch diameter hole and mount the GPS sensor into the brackets. Install weather stripping or stuffing material to prevent water and dust seepage.

Figure 1

6.2   Place the NAV-398 GPS Display mounting brackets 1 inch from the left edge of the console top and ½ inch from the front edge of the console as shown in figure 2 and enclosure 1. Mark the bracket holes using the mounting brackets as a template. Drill the holes to accept four ¾ inch 10/24 stainless 316 marine grade bolts. Drill a ½ inch hole 1-inch centered behind the mounting bracket to accept the GPS sensor cable. Mount NAV-398 display brackets to the top of the console, using lock nuts on the marine grade bolts to mount the brackets. Route the RAYSTAR sensor cable through ½ inch hole and connect it to the NAV-398 display. Install weather stripping or stuffing material to prevent water and dust seepage.

Figure 2

6.3   Power for the GPS will come from the circuit breaker panel G5-9211-00 breaker 5, as shown in figure 3. (Breaker 5 is a 5-amp breaker marked LORAN)

Figure 3

7.   **QUALITY CONTROL/QUALITY ASSURANCE:**

7.1   Care must be taken to ensure that material and installation procedures used are in accordance with references. Commanding Officers and Officers in Charge have responsibility for Quality Assurance.

8.   **SAFETY:** Use reference (b).

9.   **STABILITY IMPACT:** None

10.   **FUNDING:**

10.1   All funding for procurement of the GPS equipment shall be provided by G-OPD.

10.2   All installation funding shall be provided by each PSU.

11.   **LOGISTICS SUPPORT:** This equipment shall be installed by the servicing ESD or ESU or its equivalent for each PSU. This equipment will be supported by the ELC MICA document under APL #2AFM.

12.   **SPECIAL TOOLS/TEST EQUIPMENT:** None.

13.   **TECHNICAL MANUALS:** Use reference (b).

14.   **PREVENTIVE MAINTENANCE:** Use reference (a).

15.   **TRAINING:** Not applicable.

16.   **DOCUMENTATION:** Upon completion of this BoatAlt, the unit shall complete the bottom portion of form CG-3378 and forward as directed.

17.   **REPROCUREMENT DATA:** Not applicable.

18.   **REPAIR PROGRAM:** Not applicable.

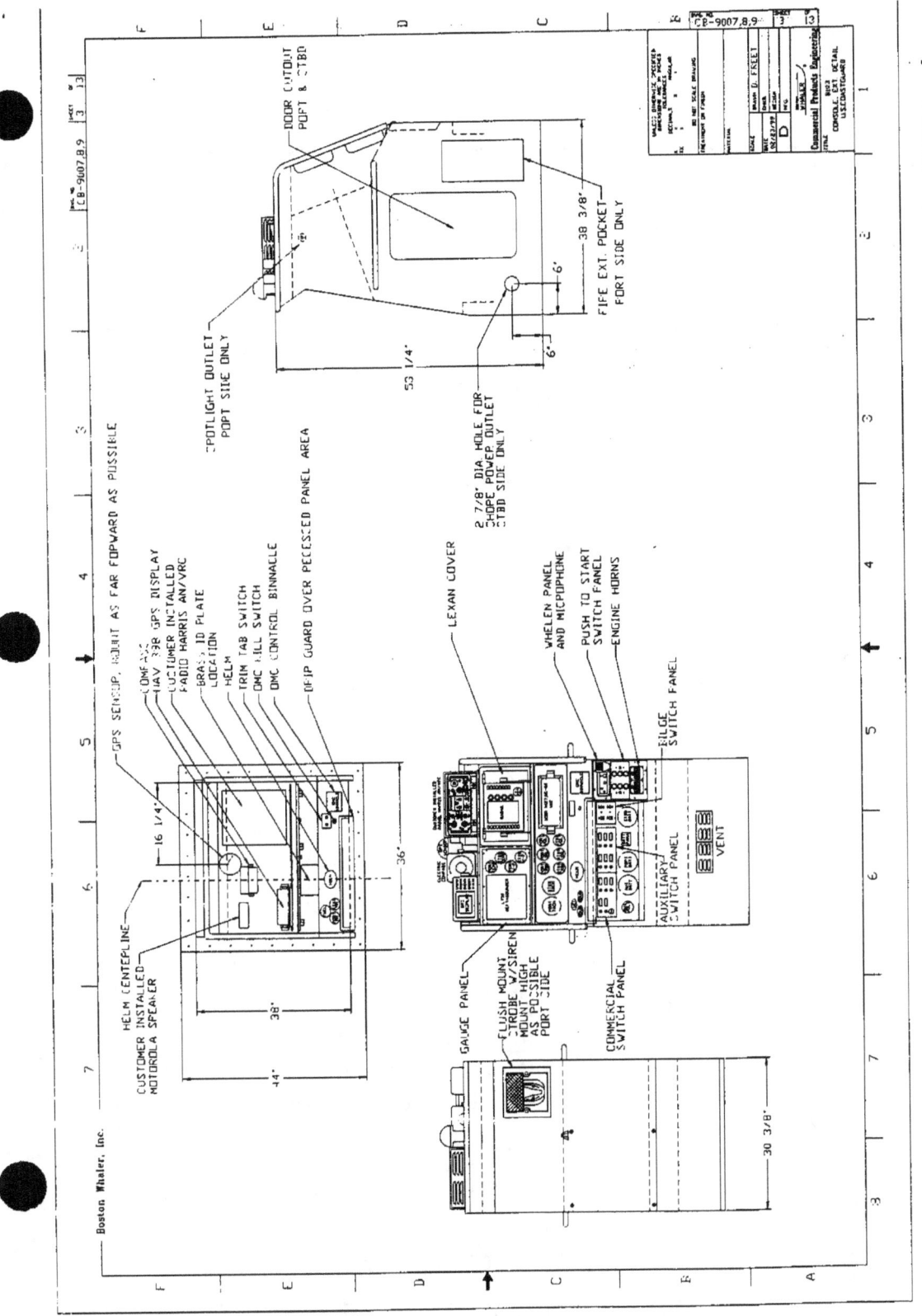

ENCLOSURE (I)

DEPARTMENT OF TRANSPORTATION U.S.COAST GUARD CG-3378 (Rev. 6-98)	BOAT ALTERATION	BOATALT NO. 25PSU-A-02
		DATE SEP 30 1999

From: Commandant, U.S. Coast Guard (G-SEN)

To: Commanders, MLCPAC(v), MLCLANT(v)

Copy To: CG PACAREA, CG LANTAREA, UTB SYS CTR, CG YARD, CG ELC, CG NMLB School, G-OCS
CG ELC (014) (016) (024) (027) G-OPD PSU (305) (307) (308) (309) (311) (313) (TRADET)

Title: Shakespeare Antenna Mount Upgrade

BoatAlt Class: A [x] B [ ] C [ ]

Haulout required: [ ] YES [x] NO

Applies to the following boats: CG PSU 25377 thru CG PSU 25384

Weight: 5 (lbs) [x] Added [ ] Removed
K.G. CHANGE +/- 00.0 (ft)

Compensation Required: (Explanation enclosed) [ ] YES [x] NO

Description:

1. Purpose: This class "A" BoatAlt directs the upgrade of the VHF-FM antenna mount. This upgrade will prevent the loss of installed antennas aboard the 25' Transportable Port Security Boat (TPSB).

R.J. FORMISANO
By Direction

DATE COMPLETED	ACTUAL COST $ _____ MAN HOURS _____
	BOAT NUMBER(S) _____

INSTRUCTIONS: A copy is sent by the MLC to the operating unit to be kept in the boat record until the BOATALT is completed. Upon completion of the BOATALT, the unit is to forward a completed and signed copy to the Group and retain a completed and signed copy in the boat record. Groups to forward in accordance with MLC SOP's.

BOAT NUMBER AND UNIT	OFFICER IN CHARGE OR COMMANDING OFFICER

PREVIOUS EDITION IS OBSOLETE

2.   Background: The current VHF-FM mount is a pleasure boat model manufactured by Shakespeare. The size of the antenna is too large for the mount and has caused many failures on the TPSB (Transportable Port Security Boat). PSU 311 has successfully prototyped the Shakespeare Model 4187-HD to replace the existing mount. The heavy-duty mount will keep the antenna secured in place at a 90-degree angle for maximum effectiveness.

3.   References:

3.1 References Already Promulgated:

(a) COMMDINST M9000.6 (series), Naval Engineering Manual
(b) COMMDINST M10550.25, Electronics Manual

3.2 References Provided by Separate Correspondence: None.

3.3 References enclosed: None.

4.   Material Required:

4.1 Shakespeare Antenna Mount 4187-HD.

5.   Equipment Removals/Relocation:

5.1 Remove the Shakespeare antenna HS-2774-1 and the mount for Shakespeare antenna Motorola Spectra radio from the radar mast.

6.   Equipment Installations.

6.1 Install the new Shakespeare Antenna Mount 4187-HD in the same location as the old antenna mount. Re-install the Shakespeare HS-2774-1 antenna into the new heavy-duty mount.

7.   Quality Control/Quality Assurance: Care must be taken to ensure the material and the installation procedures are in accordance with references. Commanding Officers and Officers in Charges have responsibility for Quality Assurance.

8.   Safety: None

9.   Stability Impact: None

10.   Funding:

10.1 The material and installation cost shall be funded by the units using AFC-Funds.

10.2 Cost Estimate:
Materials:$33.57 per hull
Labor: 2 hours per hull

11. **Parts Support:** N/A.

12. **Special Tools/Test Equipment:** None.

13. **Technical Manual/Drawings:** None.

14. **Preventive Maintenance:** None.

15. **Training:** N/A.

16. **Documentation:** G-OPD shall update the OLSP and ELC shall update the MICA documentation.

17. **Procurement Data:** Coast Guard price is $33.57 each.

The Shakespeare Company
19845 U. S. Highway 76
P.O. Box 733
Newberry, SC 29108-9803.
Telephone: (803) 276-5504
Marine/Sales & Marketing

18. **Repair Program:** None.

Appendix B
WIRING DIAGRAMS

Introduction	This reference contains wiring diagrams for various components on the 25' TPSB.		
In this Appendix			
	Section	**Title**	**See Page**
	A	Auxiliary Switch Panel	B-2
	B	Battery Switch and Parallel Switch Wiring	B-3
	C	Dual Bilge Pump Panel	B-4
	D	Distribution Bus Wiring Diagram	B-5
	E	Battery Charger and Shore Power	B-6
	F	Electronics Distribution Panel	B-7
	G	Console Fuse Block	B-8
	H	Commercial Switch Panel	B-9
	I	Push to Start Panel	B-10

THIS PAGE LEFT INTENTIONALLY BLANK

BOSTON WHALER   25' U.S.C.G. Trailerable Port Security Boat (25' TPSB)

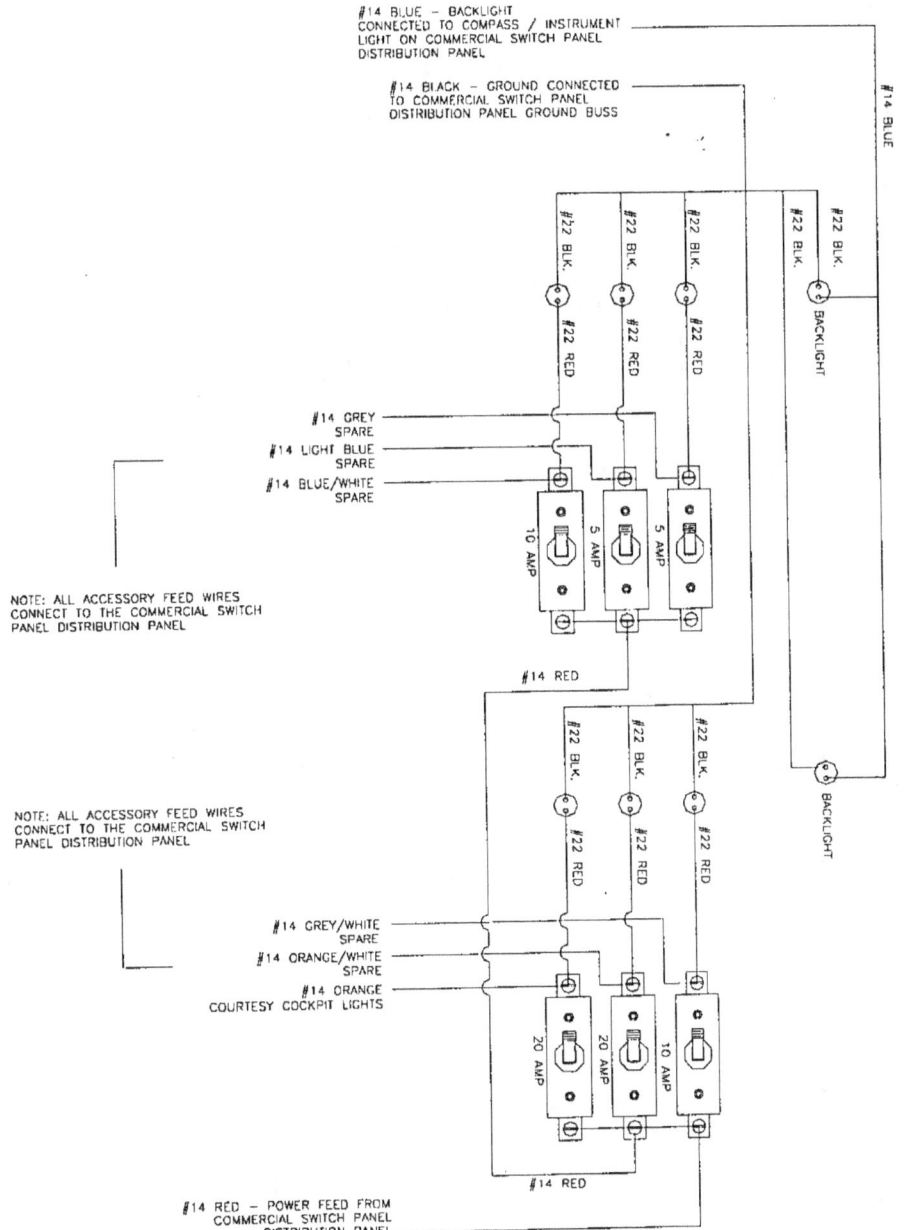

AUXILIARY SWITCH PANEL WIRING DIAGRAM

BOSTON WHALER   25' U.S.C.G. Trailerable Port Security Boat (25' TPSB)

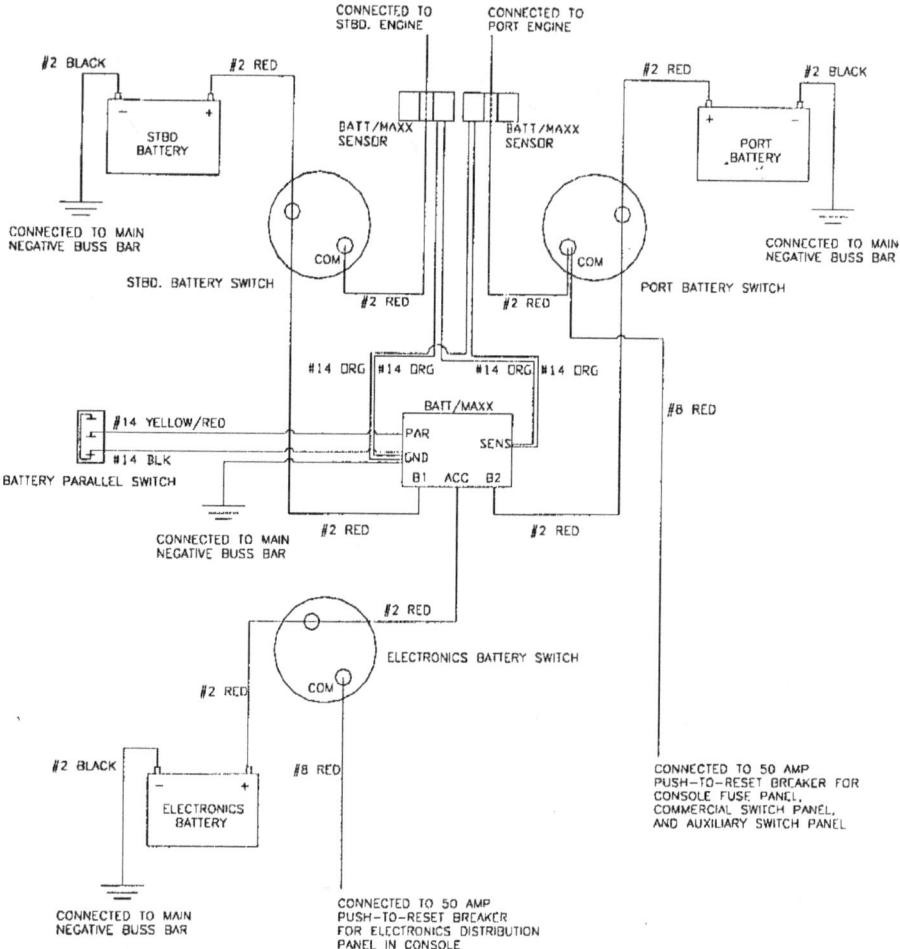

BATTERY SWITCH & PARALLEL SWITCH WIRING DIAGRAM

BOSTON WHALER   25' U.S.C.G. Trailerable Port Security Boat (25' TPSB)

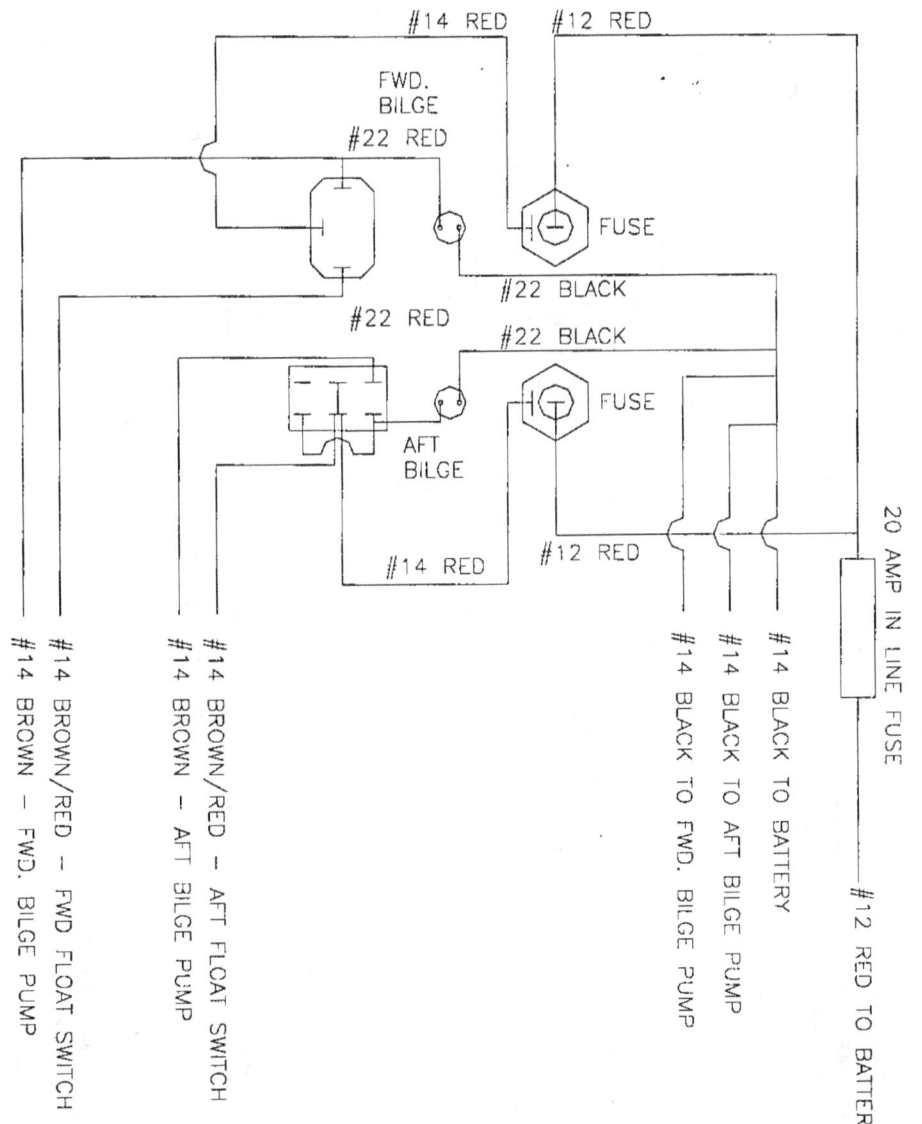

DUAL BILGE PUMP PANEL WIRING DIAGRAM

BOSTON WHALER

25' U.S.C.G. Trailerable Port Security Boat (25' TPSB)

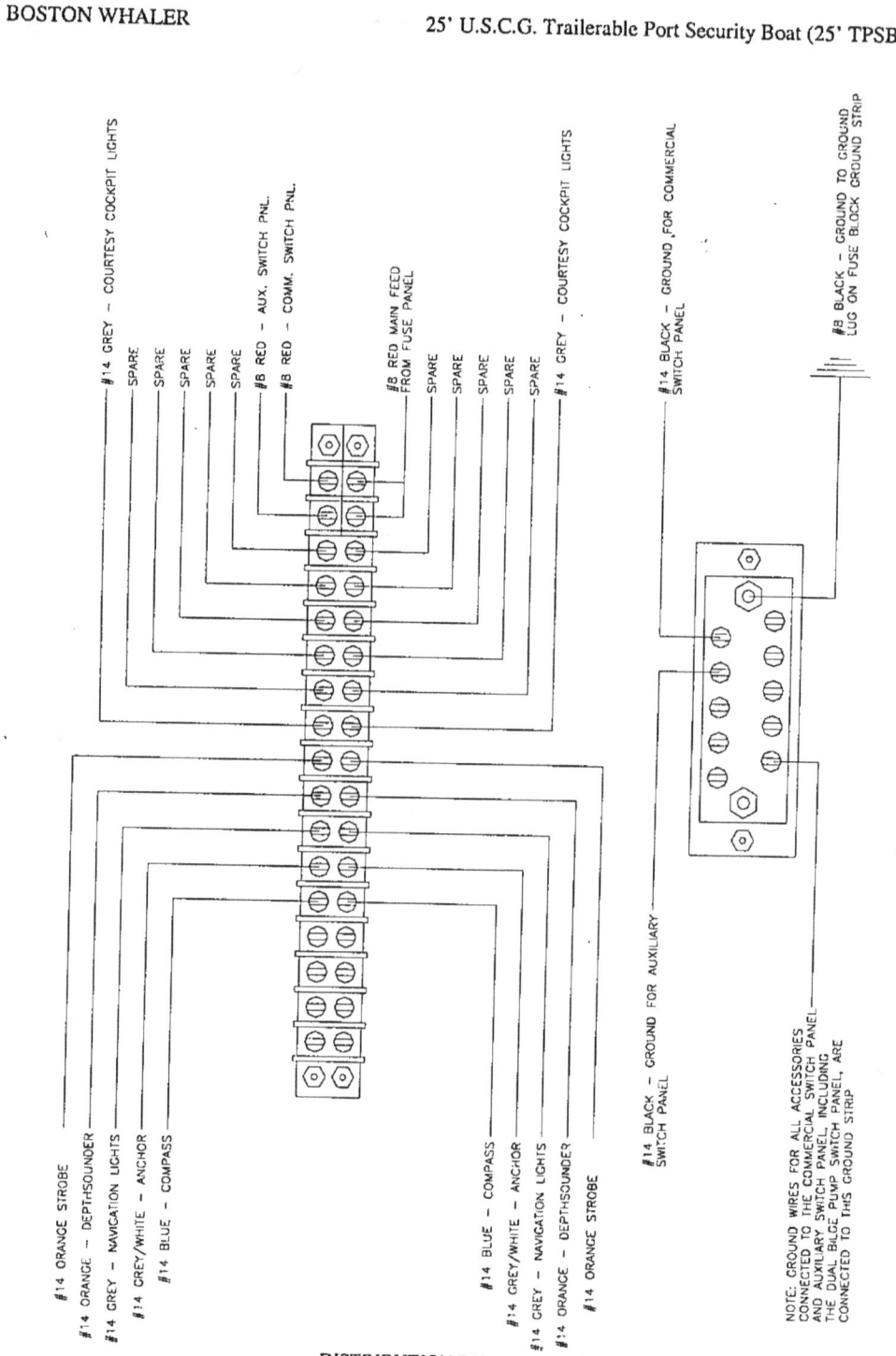

DISTRIBUTION BUSS WIRING DIAGRAM

NOTE: GROUND WIRES FOR ALL ACCESSORIES
CONNECTED TO THE COMMERCIAL SWITCH PANEL
AND AUXILIARY SWITCH PANEL INCLUDING
THE DUAL BILGE PUMP SWITCH PANEL, ARE
CONNECTED TO THIS GROUND STRIP

BOSTON WHALER   25' U.S.C.G. Trailerable Port Security Boat (25' TPSB)

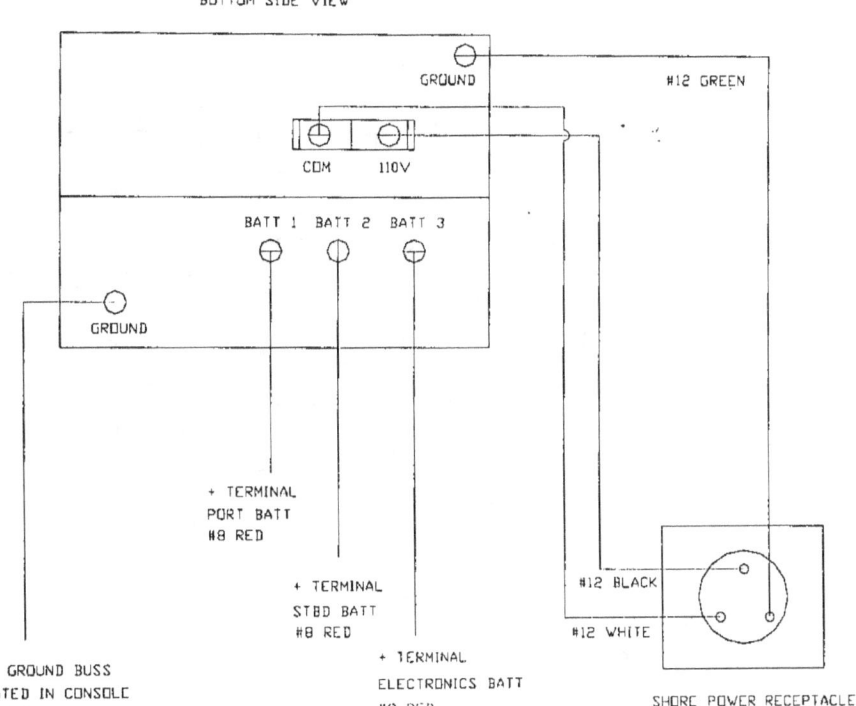

BATTERY CHARGER & SHORE POWER WIRING DIAGRAM

BOSTON WHALER
25' U.S.C.G. Trailerable Port Security Boat (25' TPSB)

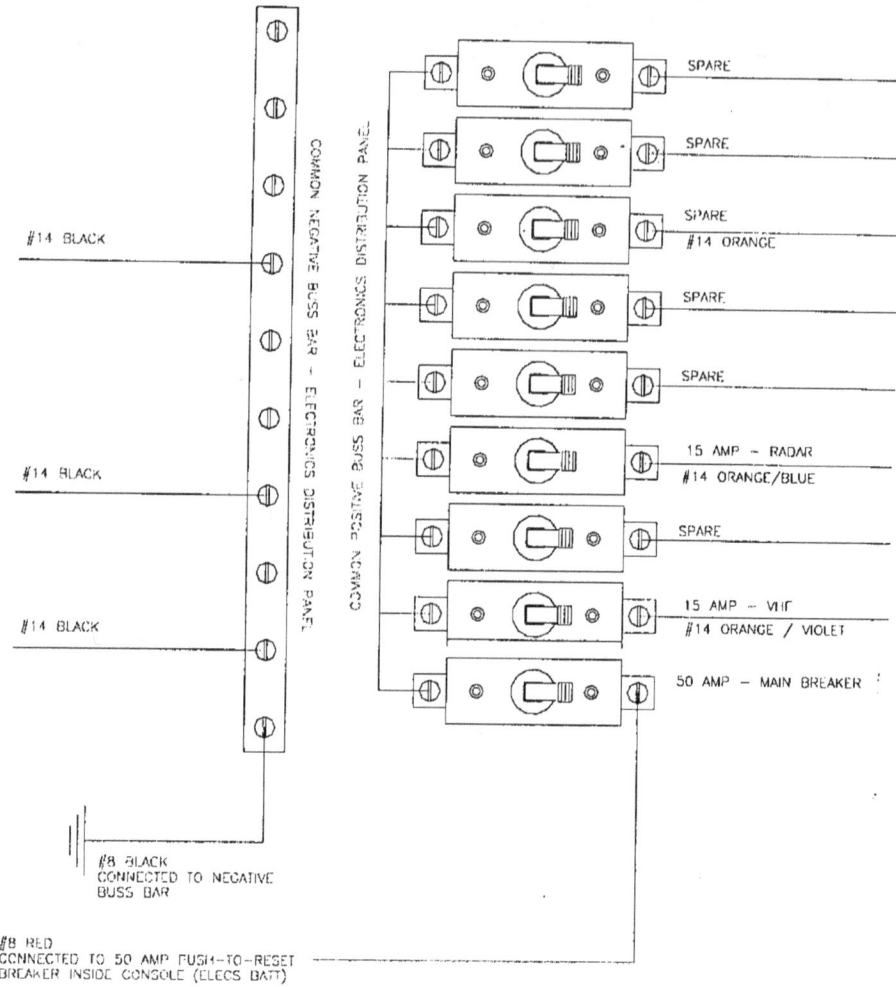

ELECTRONICS DISTRIBUTION PANEL WIRING DIAGRAM

BOSTON WHALER   25' U.S.C.G. Trailerable Port Security Boat (25' TPSB)

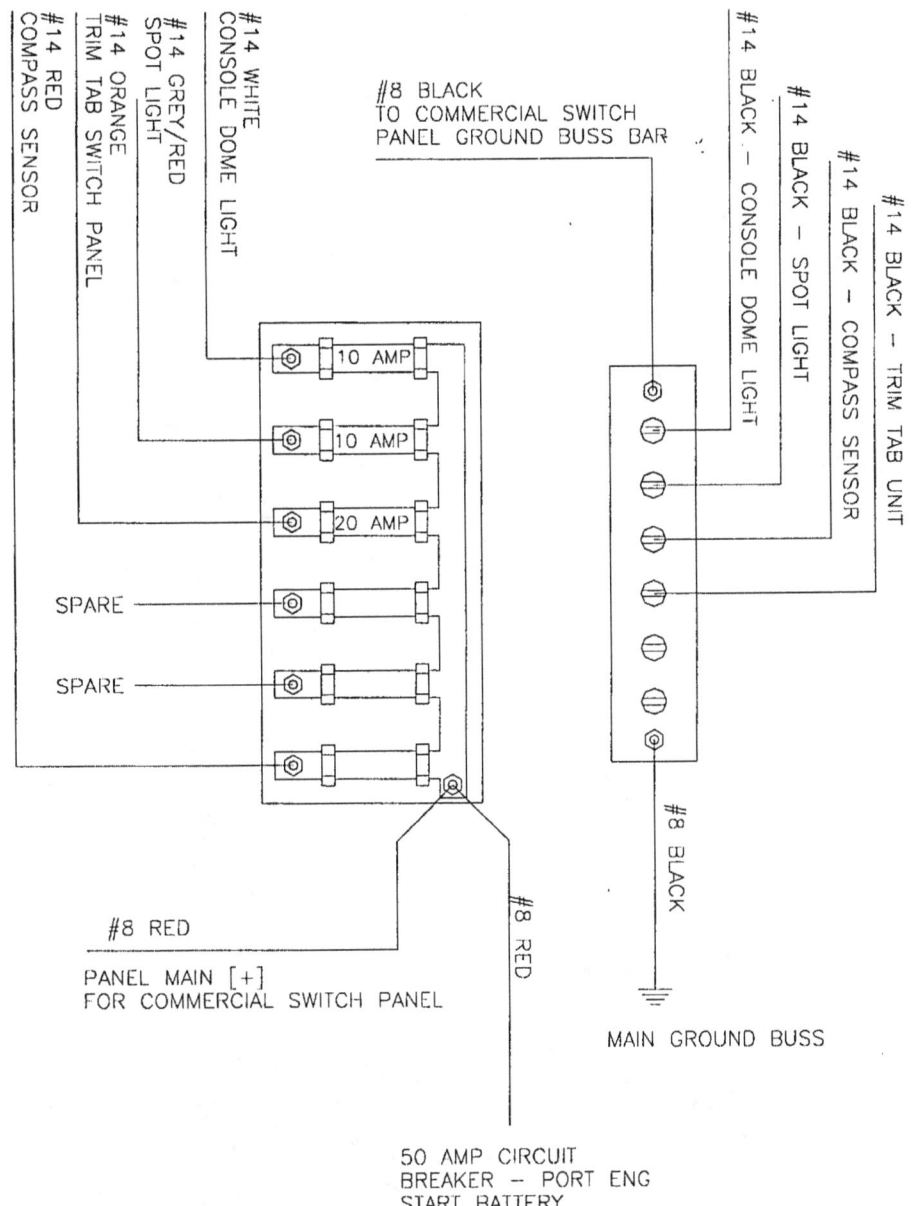

FIGURE 2 - CONSOLE FUSE BLOCK WIRING DIAGRAM

6

BOSTON WHALER   25' U.S.C.G. Trailerable Port Security Boat (25' TPSB)

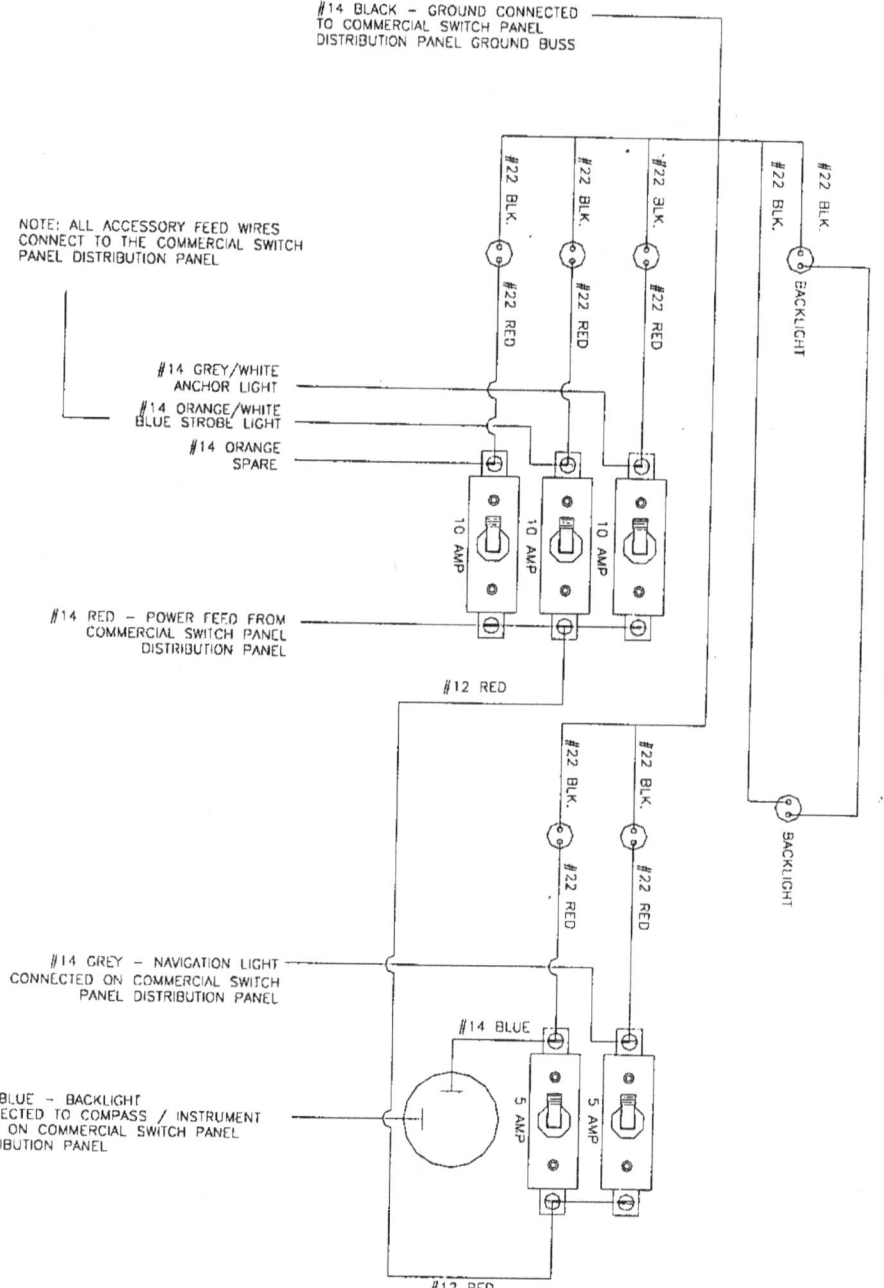

COMMERCIAL SWITCH PANEL WIRING DIAGRAM

BOSTON WHALER   25' U.S.C.G. Trailerable Port Security Boat (25' TPSB)

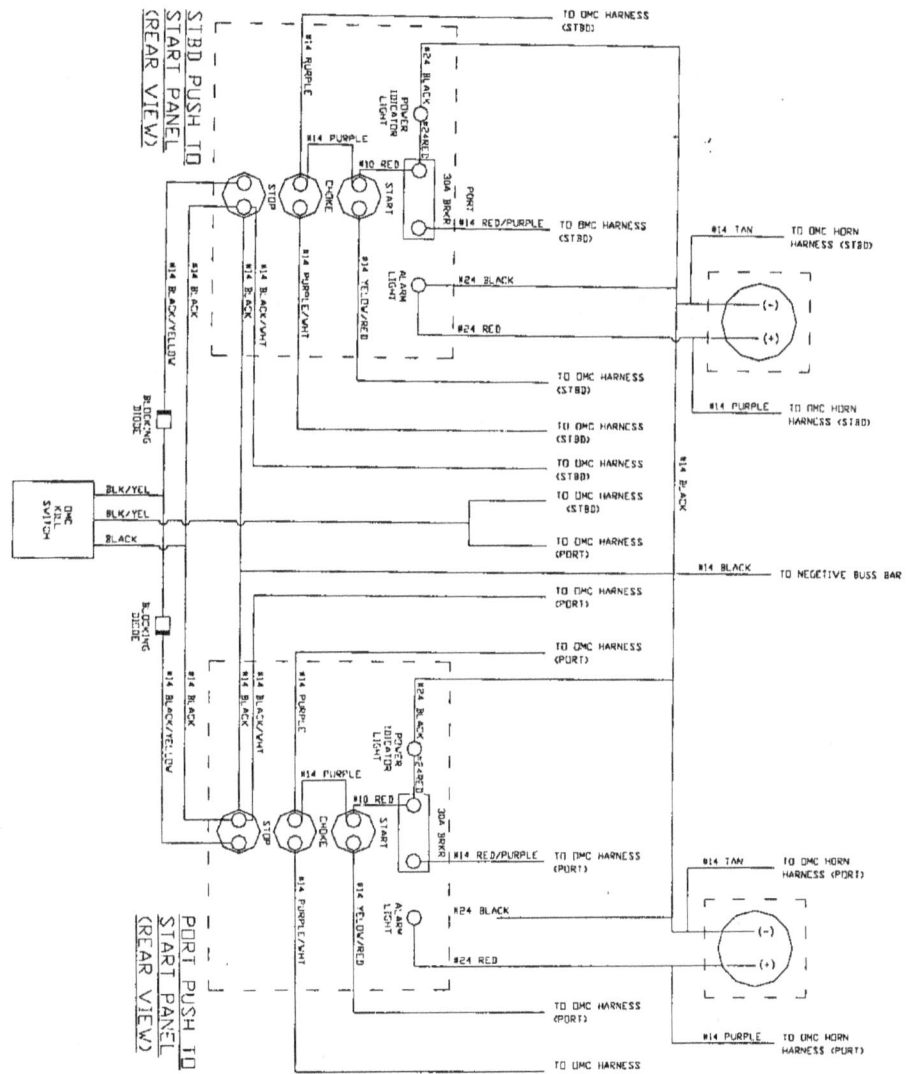

PUSH-TO-START PANEL WIRING DIAGRAM

Appendix C 25' TPSB ELECTRONIC OPERATOR'S GUIDE	
Overview	
Introduction	This appendix contains guides to TPSB electronics operations.

THIS PAGE LEFT INTENTIONALLY BLANK

Digital Display Operation (MD-100)

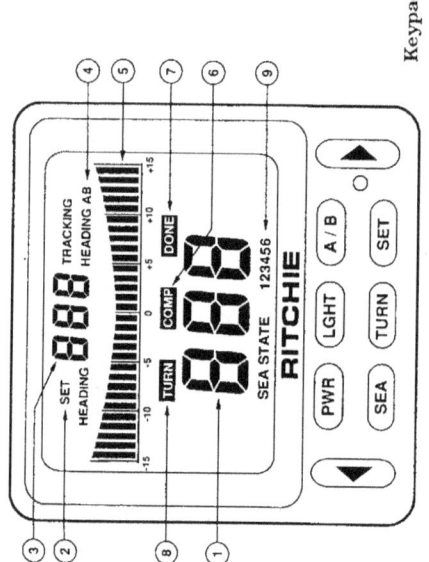

1. HEADING DISPLAY: Displays the vessel's heading.
2. SET HEADING: Flashes to indicate no heading has been set into memory.
3. HEADING MEMORY DISPLAY: Displays the headings that have been set into memory.
4. HEADING MEMORY INDICATOR: Displays memory heading selected—A or B.
5. OFF COURSE INDICATOR: Indicates the vessel is heading off course, up to 15° port (–) or starboard (+).
6. COMP: Indicates auto-compensation procedure is in process.
7. DONE: Indicates auto-compensation has been completed correctly.
8. TURN: Indicates temporary sea state damping in effect to eliminate lag in turns.
9. SEA STATE: Indicates level of damping of heading data. Default setting is 3.

Keypad Functions

PWR — Press once for on; press again for off.

LGHT — Backlight LCD—press once for low light, again for high light, again for OFF.

A/B — Press to select "A" or "B" memory. Selection indicated in upper right corner of LCD. See SET, below.

SEA — Press to adjust damping for sea state.

TURN — Temporarily (20 seconds) bypasses the sea state damping while making a turn to reduce lag in heading readout. To turn OFF, wait 20 seconds, press second time or press SET when reaching desired heading.

SET — Press to set bearing into memory, A or B, and activate Off Course Indicator.

▲ ▼ — Scroll keys to adjust a heading in memory. See example.

○ — Auto-Compensation Key. Push to activate, using pointed object. See page 6.

To Put a Second Heading (342°) into Memory

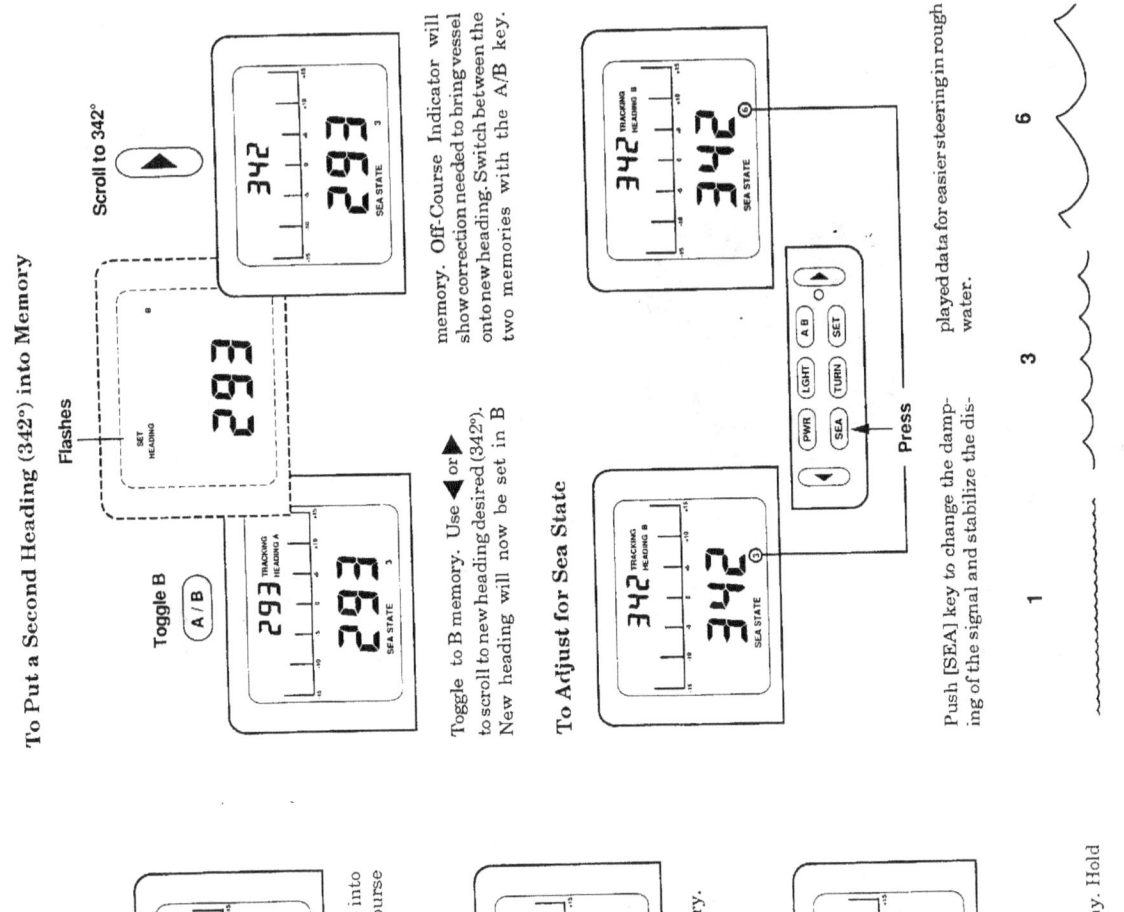

Scroll to 342°

Flashes

Toggle B

memory. Off-Course Indicator will show correction needed to bring vessel onto new heading. Switch between the two memories with the A/B key.

Toggle to B memory. Use ▲ or ▼ to scroll to new heading desired (342°). New heading will now be set in B memory.

To Adjust for Sea State

Press

Push [SEA] key to change the damping of the signal and stabilize the displayed data for easier steering in rough water.

Operating Examples

Setting a Course

Flashes

SET

Steer vessel on the desired course, as shown on digital heading display. Then press [SET]. This will put course into memory and activate the Off-Course Indicator.

Using the Off-Course Indicator

Steer to Center

5° left of course set in memory. Steer to starboard

8° right of course set in memory. Steer to port

To Adjust Course

Increase

Decrease

Press the arrow keys to increase or decrease the Heading Memory Display. Hold down to scroll.

Compass (Analog) Display Operation (MD-200)

The Ritchie MD-200 MagTronic display combines the traditional appearance of a compass card with a digital readout. The dial provides an easy reference for steering. The digital readout provides a precise numerical reference for use in navigation.

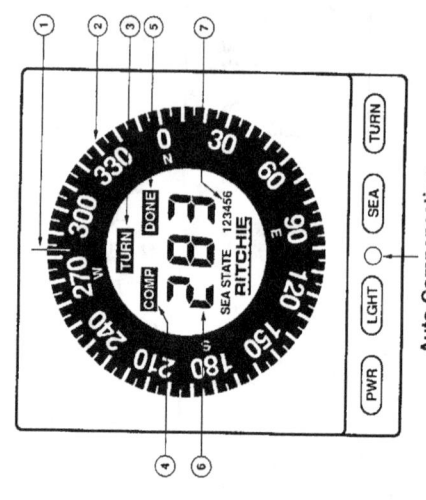

Auto-Compensation

1. LUBBER LINE
2. COMPASS CARD: shows vessel's heading.
3. TURN: indicates temporary sea state damping in effect to eliminate lag in turns.
4. COMP: indicates auto-compensation in process.
5. DONE: auto-compensation completed.
6. HEADING DISPLAY: displays vessel's heading.
7. SEA STATE: indicates level of damping of heading data. Default setting is 3.

Keypad Functions

PWR Press once for on; press again for off.

LGHT Backlighting for compass card and digital readout. Press once for low light, again for high light, again for off.

○ Push to activate automatic compensation. Use pointed object. See page 6.

SEA Press to select sea state setting.

TURN Press before making turn. Temporarily (20 seconds) bypasses sea state damping to reduce lag in digital readout and compass card. To turn off, wait 20 seconds or press second time.

To Eliminate Readout Lag in a Turn

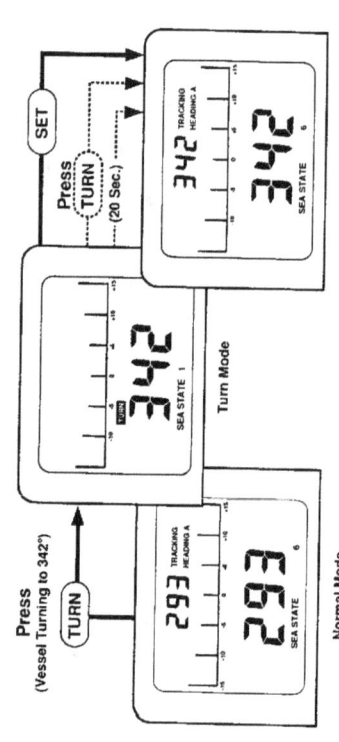

Press
(Vessel Turning to 342°)

Press [TURN] and for 20 seconds Sea State is reduced to 1 to eliminate lag in the digital readout during a turn. The

Turn mode can be cancelled by pressing [TURN] again or by pressing [SET] when new course is reached.

Using Off-Course Indicator for Sailing

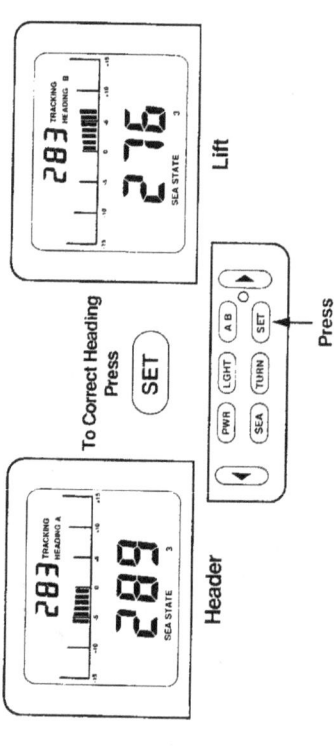

When sailing to windward, you can set the close hauled course into memory and then use the Off Course Indicator to detect headers or lifts. On starboard tack, going off course (up slope) to the left (minus) indicates a header, up

slope to the right, a lift. On port tack it is the opposite. A corrected heading can be quickly SET into memory, and the above process continued. Laylines, leeway, and downwind shifts can also be checked in a similar process.

Trouble-Shooting Guide

Symptom	Possible Cause(s)	Things to Check
Display will not turn on	Bad connections, Blown fuse, Circuit breaker trip	Check all power connections, Check fuse, Reset breaker
Display flashes 888s at power ON and then goes blank.	No data from sensor	**Check power to sensor.** **Check connections between sensor and display. Sensor is located near extreme magnet interference.**
Display goes blank during normal operation.	Interference from other electrical hardware.	Connect power directly to battery.
Display flashes 888s and returns to normal operation.	Intermittent data from sensor.	Check power to sensor. Check connections.
Erroneous heading data	Deviation of vessel has changed since Auto-Comp	Repeat Auto-Comp procedure
	Tools or other metal objects placed near sensor	"
	Lightning	"
	Sensor not level in bracket	Adjust to level, Tighten thumbscrews
Constant error— Example: (Always Off + 10°)	Sensor loose in clamping ring (Not parallel to centerline)	Align with vessel centerline and tighten clamping ring
Display flashes **Err** during compensation	Compensation error	Compensation rule violated. Repeat compensation procedure more carefully.

Note: Most problems are the result of faulty connections. If problems persist, contact Ritchie Technical Dealer or Ritchie Customer Service.

Operating Examples

To Steer a Course (283°)

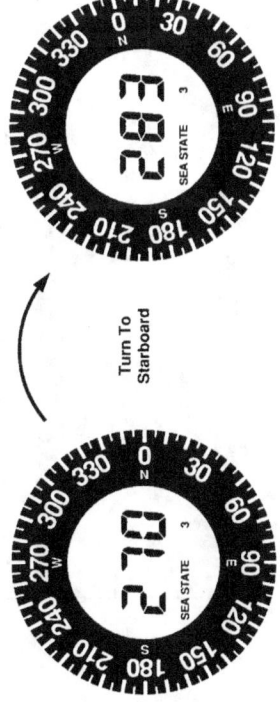

Turn To Starboard

Use the compass card for reference, and always turn towards the course you want to steer—the same as with a flat dial on a magnetic compass.

To Adjust for Sea State

SEA

Increment [SEA] key to change the damping of the signal and stabilize the displayed data for easier steering in rough water.

To Eliminate Readout Lag in a Turn

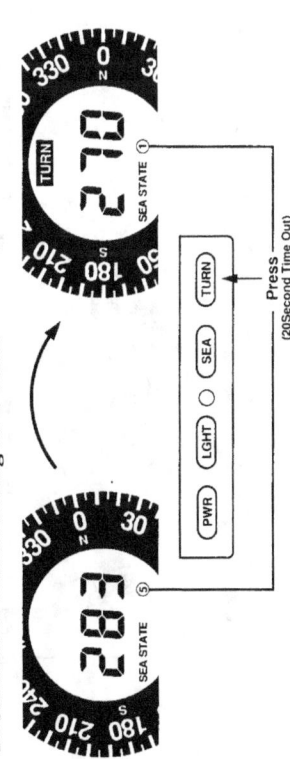

PWR LGHT ○ SEA TURN

← Press (20 Second Time Out)

Press [TURN] and for 20 seconds Sea State damping filter is bypassed to eliminate lag in compass card and digital readout during a turn. Turn mode can be cancelled by pressing [TURN] again.

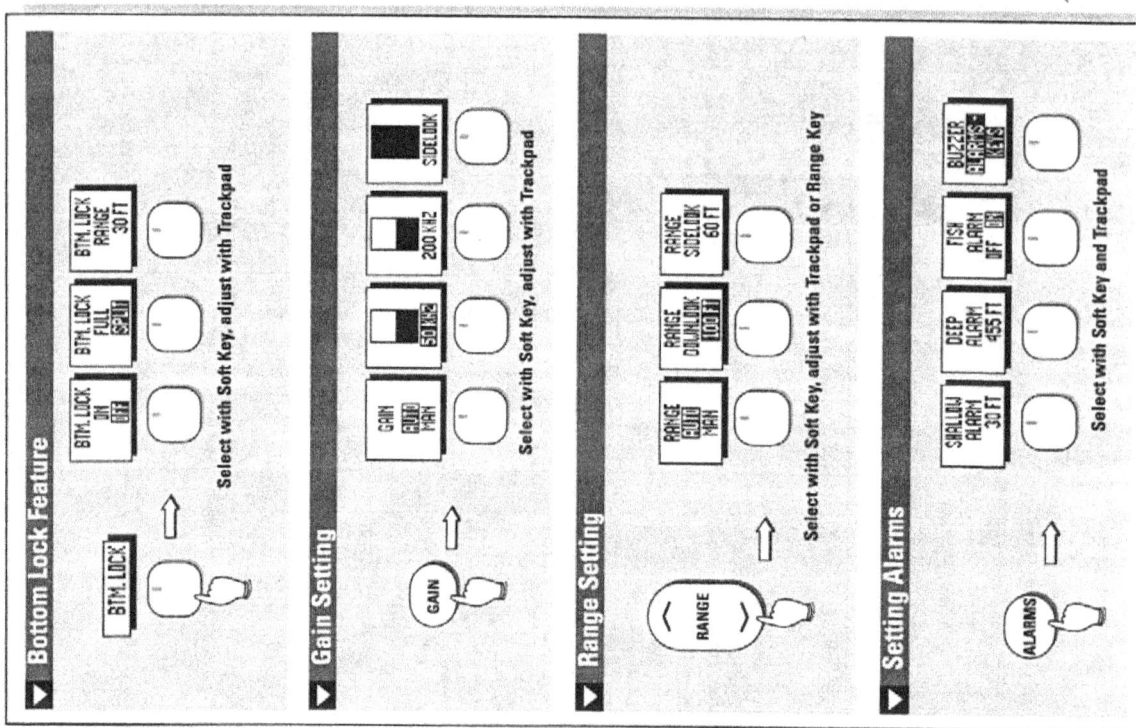

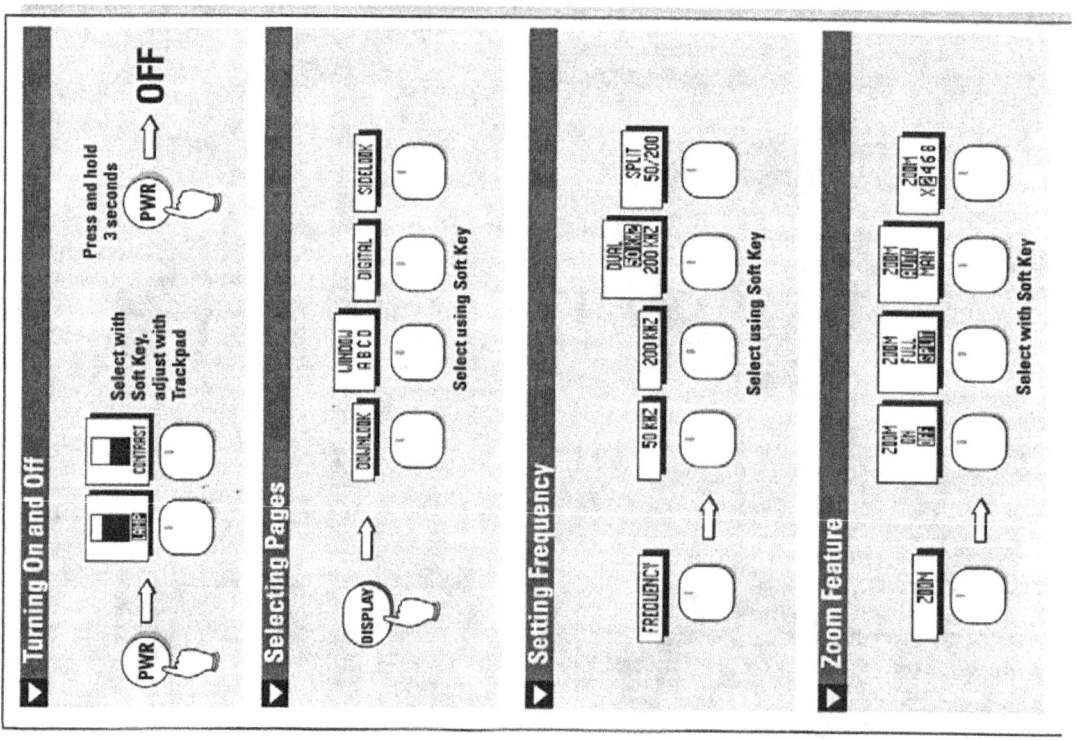

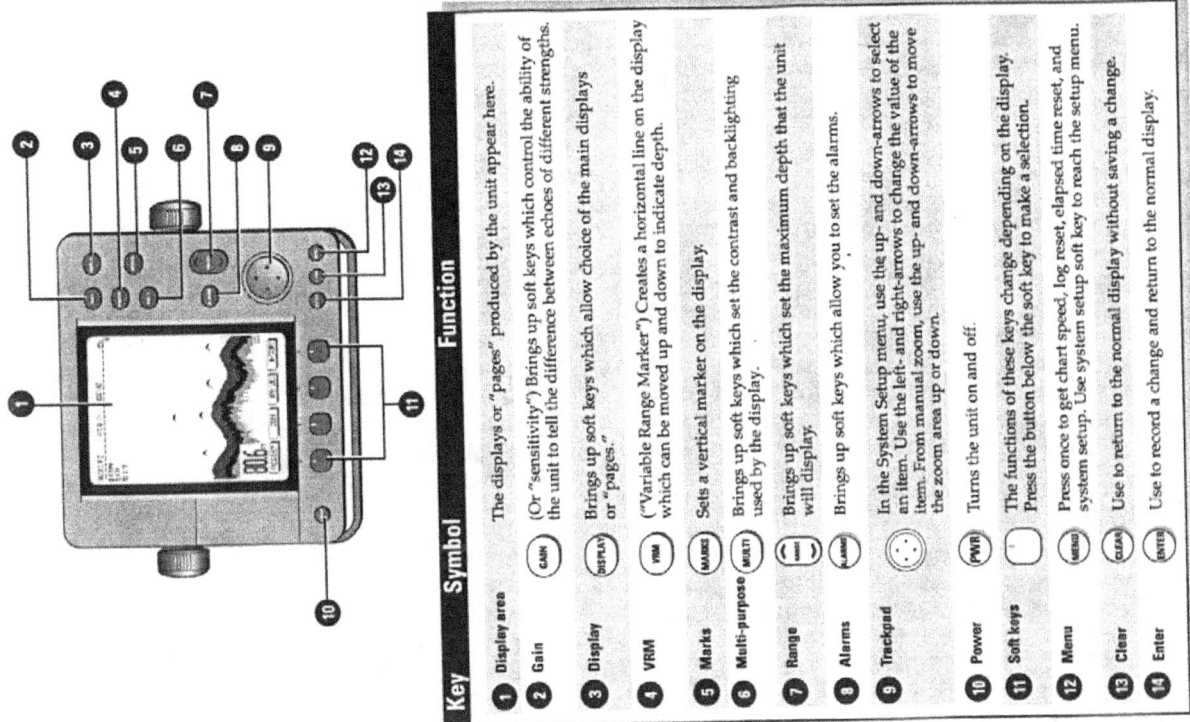

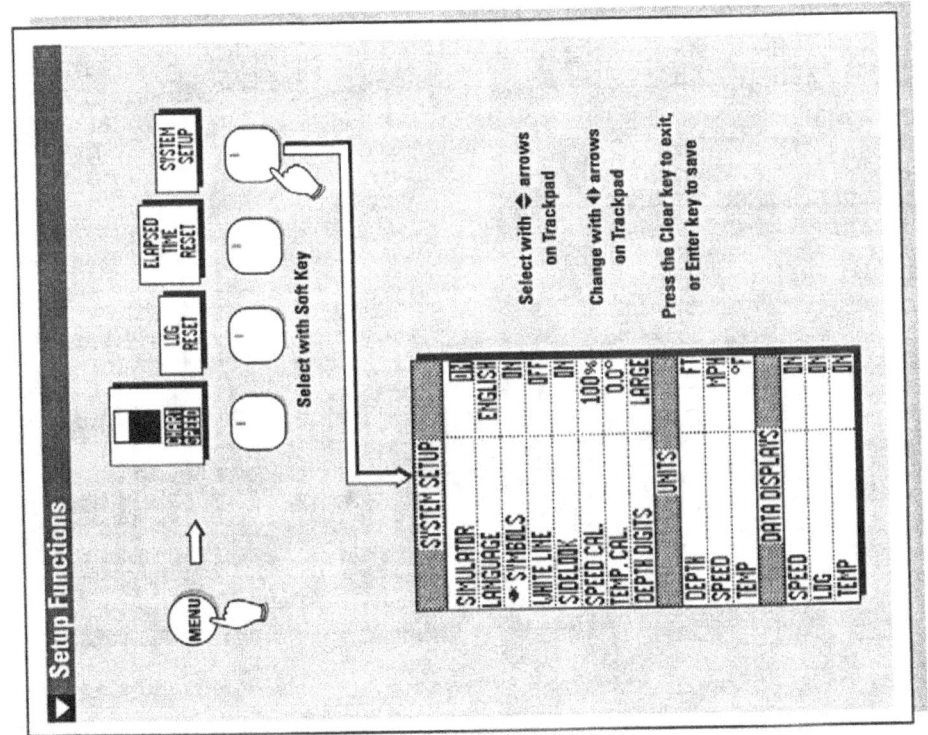

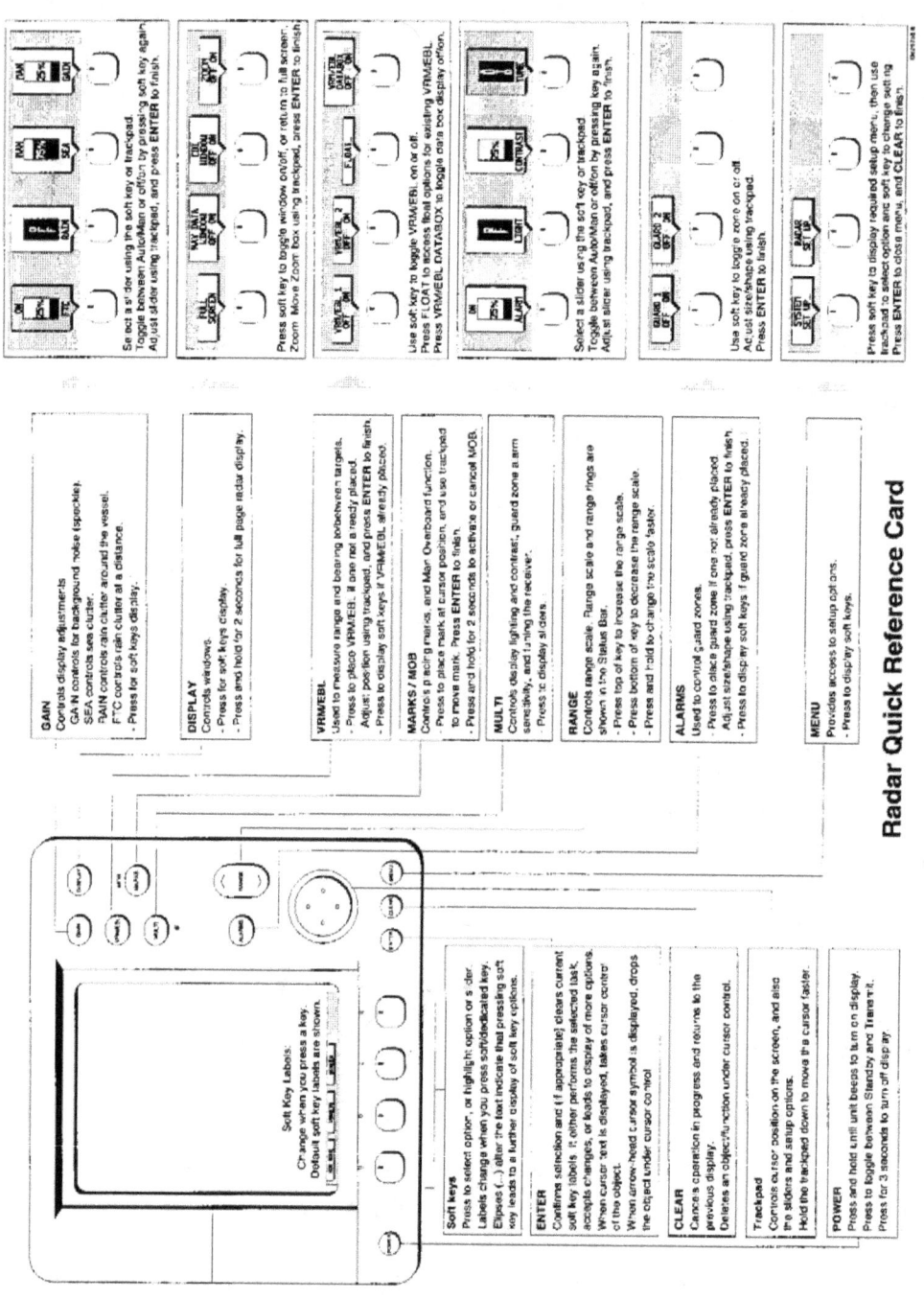

Radar Quick Reference Card

Default Soft Keys

HDG MODE

| NORTH UP | COURSE UP | HEAD UP | Only displayed if heading available. |

Press the required soft key to change the heading mode, and press ENTER

TARGETS

| INT REJ | EXPANSION | WAKES | TARGETS |
| OFF ON | OFF ON | OFF S M L | DAY NIGHT |

Press the WAKES soft key until the required option (short, medium or long wakes, or OFF) is highlighted.
Press the other soft keys to toggle Interference Rejection or Target Expansion on/off, or Target presentation between day and night.
Press ENTER to accept.

SCREEN

| CRSR BOX | RNGE RNGS | DATA BOXES | WAYPOINT |
| OFF ON | OFF ON | OFF ON | OFF ON |

Press the appropriate soft key to toggle on/off Cursor Readout Databox or Waypoint display and press ENTER to accept.

Context Sensitive Cursor Control

When the cursor is positioned over special features on the display, a text label appears to identify the feature. Depending on the feature, you can then move, re-size or delete it.

Text Label	Feature
BOX	Data box (any type)
CTR	Radar centre
EBL	Electronic Bearing Line
FLT	Floating VRM/EBL
GRD	Guard zone corner or side
MRK	Mark
SHM	Ship's Heading Marker
VRM	Variable Range Marker
VRM/EBL	VRM and EBL
ZMB	Zoom box

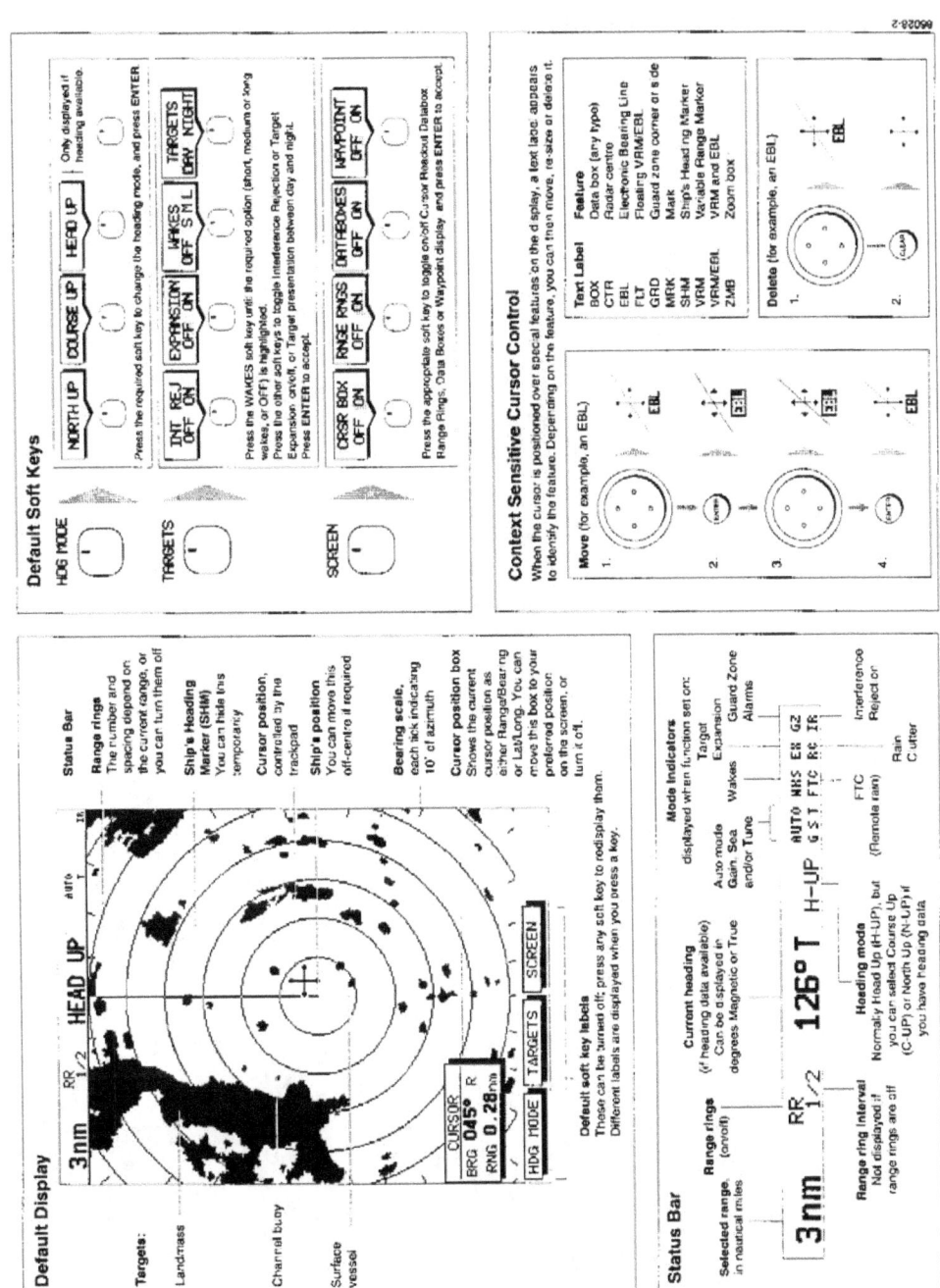

Default Display

Targets:

Landmass

Channel buoy

Surface vessel

Status Bar

Range rings
The number and spacing depend on the current range, or you can turn them off

Ship's Heading Marker (SHM)
You can hide this temporarily

Cursor position, controlled by the trackpad

Ship's position
You can move this off-centre if required

Bearing scale, each tick indicating 10° of azimuth

Cursor position box
Shows the current cursor position as either Range/Bearing or Lat/Long. You can move this box to your preferred position on the screen, or turn it off.

Default soft key labels
These can be turned on/off: press any soft key to redisplay them. Different labels are displayed when you press a key.

Status Bar

Selected range, in nautical miles

Range rings (on/off)

Range ring interval
Not displayed if range rings are off

Current heading
(if heading data available)
Can be displayed in degrees Magnetic or True

Heading mode
Normally Head Up (H-UP), but you can select Course Up (C-UP) or North Up (N-UP) if you have heading data

Mode Indicators
displayed when function set on:

Auto mode Gain Sea and/or Tune — Wakes — Target Expansion — Guard Zone Alarms

FTC (Remote rain) — Rain Clutter — Interference Reject or

AUTO WKS EX G2
G S T FTC RC IR

Appendix D
25' TPSB OUTFIT LIST

Overview	
Introduction	This appendix is the standard 25' TPSB Outfit List.

THIS PAGE LEFT INTENTIONALLY BLANK

Description	U/I	Quantity

25' Transportable Port Security Boat (TPSB) heavy duty fiberglass laminate with aluminum inserts.
 	
    Navy grey gel-coat
 	
    Haze grey gel-coat
 	
    30" Reinforced Transom
	EA	1

Anchor, 14 lbs. Danforth	EA	1
Anchor 5' Chain w/swivel, 150' 1-1/4" 3-strand Nylon Line	EA	1
Antenna Base	EA	1
Antenna Bracket	EA	1
Antenna, Shakespeare 4242 VHF	EA	1
Antenna, Shakespeare, 4265A VHF	EA	1
Antenna, Shakespeare, 4310 UHF	EA	1
Antenna, VHF-FM	EA	1
Bag, Watertight	EA	1
Battery, 750 CCA 12V Marine, 105 amp. EMDE, Model NG-27, VCI Group 27	EA	3
Battery Charger, 50 Amp, 4 Bank w/ Shore Power Cord & Receptacle	EA	1
Battery, Emergency Parallel Switch	EA	1
Battery Isolator Switch	EA	3
Battery Switch Instructions	EA	1
Bilge Pump, Electric 500 GPH w/ manual/ auto control in forward below deck stowage	EA	1
Bilge Pump, Electric 1000 GPH w/ manual/ auto control in aft bilge (1 port, 1 starboard)	EA	2
Bilge Pump, Float Switch	EA	3
Binoculars, 8 x 50	EA	1
Boat Hook, Telescopic	EA	1
Boots, Fireman's Waterproof, Thermal Insulated (17.5")	PR	
Bow Eye, Heavy Duty Extended Reinforced	EA	1
Canopy/Sun Tent w/ gray canvas	EA	1
Console, Aluminum including aluminum doors, aluminum grab rails, removable gauge panel, radio box, and radar display compartment	EA	1

Description	U/I	Quantity
Console, Bilge Pump, Dual Switch Panel	EA	1
Console, Switch Panel, 5 toggle/breakers w/dimmer switch	EA	1
Console, Switch Panel, Accessory, 6 Toggle/Breakers	EA	1
Compass, Navigation, Magnetic	EA	1
Compass, w/ Remote Sensor, Richie MC-200B	EA	1
Cover, 25'	EA	1
Cutwater, Stainless Steel	EA	1
Deck Cleats, 10" Deck	EA	7
Deck Hatch, 12" x 15" Oval Aluminum	EA	1
Deck Tie Downs, Recessed	EA	2
Depth Sounder, Raytheon L750	EA	1
Distribution Panel, Electronics	EA	1
Engine, Long Shaft CIVIC 175 HP V-6 FICHT	EA	2
Engine, Emergency Ignition Cutoff Switch	EA	1
Engine, OMC Equipment Package, Dual Outboard	EA	1
Engine, Flusher	EA	1
Engine, Horn, Warning Kit 585149, 585992	EA	1
Gauge, Engine Hour meter	EA	2
Gauge, Engine Tachometer including, Low VRO, temperature, service lights	EA	2
Gauge, Engine Tilt & Trim	EA	2
Gauge, Engine Water Pressure	EA	2
Gauge, Engine Voltmeter	EA	3
Gauge, Fuel	EA	1
Engine, Dual Throttle w/ trim control	EA	1
Engine, Shift/Throttle Mechanical Cables (Port) 24'	EA	1
Engine, Shift/Throttle Mechanical Cables (Stbd) 22'	EA	1
Engine Oil(VRO) Injection System, 3.0 gal	EA	1
Ensign, National	EA	1
Ensign, Coast Guard	EA	1
Fender, Gray 8" x 30"	EA	4
Fire Extinguisher, Type 1 Dry Chemical	EA	1
Footrest	EA	1
Fuel Supply Line, 3/8" ID Type A Hose	EA	2
Fuel Supply Filter/Water Separators	EA	2
Fuel Supply Line Bayonet Style Connector	EA	2
Fuel Tank, 171 Gal Aluminum	EA	1
Fuel Tank, Filler Reinforced Rubber Hose	EA	1
Fuel Tank, Filler "Gas" Plate	EA	1
Fuel Tank Vent Tube, 5/8"	EA	1

Description	U/I	Quantity
Grapple, Hook	EA	1
Grapple, 5' Chain, 150' 3/4" Three Strand Nylon Line	EA	1
Gun Mount,.50 cal, MK 93	EA	1
Gun Mount, Stand Assy. MK 16 Mod 8	EA	3
Gun Mount, M240B, MK 82, Mod 2	EA	2
Gunwales, Aluminum	EA	1
Ignition Panel, Push-to-start Dual Engine	EA	1
Leaning Post, Aluminum w/ rifle & ammunition storage	EA	1
Light, Console Courtesy	EA	1
Light, Navigation, Mast	EA	1
Light, Navigation, Mast Bulbs	EA	1
Light, Navigation, Running, Port	EA	1
Light, Navigation, Running, Starboard	EA	1
Light, Spotlight, Hand Held	EA	1
Light, 6" Blue Strobe, Whalen Model 800 CHBP	EA	1
Line, Mooring, 25'	EA	4
Line, Mooring 5/8" 3-strand Nylon (25' & 15')		
Lifting Eyes, Stainless Steel	EA	4
Loud Hailer, PA Set, AN/PIQ-5	EA	1
Navigation, Global Positioning System, Raytheon Marine NAV-398 Raytheon Marine RAYSTAR-112	EA	1
Navigation Kit	KT	1
Navigation, Nautical Slide Rule	EA	1
Night Vision Goggles, AN/PVS-7C	EA	1
Plug, Boat	EA	4
Pour Spout	EA	1
Radar Set, Raytheon L74	EA	1
Radio, Motorola Spectra	EA	1
Radio, AN/PRC 117 Triband	EA	1
Rail, Cockpit Lashing	EA	2
Rail, Heavy Duty Rub	EA	1
Rail, Rubbing Strakes (2 ea side)	EA	4
Rail, Lo Pattern	EA	2
Rail, Aluminum Engine Crash	EA	1
Safety, Air Horn	EA	1
Safety, First Aid Kit	EA	1
Safety, Radar Reflector, Collapsible	EA	1
Safety, Paddle	EA	2
Safety, Pall, Collapsible	EA	1
Scupper, Cockpit	EA	2
Splashwell Bulkhead, Fiberglas	EA	1

Description	U/I	Quantity
Survival, Boat Crew Kit	EA	4
Survival, Light, Marker, Distress, SDU-5	EA	4
Survival, Line Stoppers (Life Vests)	EA	1
Survival, PFD, Type III, Gray or Black	EA	6
Survival, Ring Buoy	EA	1
Survival, Signal Mirror	EA	4
Survival Suit, Dry Suit	EA	9
Survival Suit, Mustang	EA	9
Survival, Throw Bag with Floating Line	EA	1
Steering, Twin Hydraulic Cylinder, Teleflex HC5342	EA	1
Steering, Hydraulic Hoses	FT	24
Steering/Helm, 16" Black Stainless Steel	EA	1
Steering/Helm Pump w/bezel	EA	1
Steering, Tie Bar & Engine Adapter Plates	EA	1
Stern Eyes, Stainless Steel	EA	2
Strobe & Siren, Flush mount	EA	1
Tool, Kit	SE	1
Tool, Gas Filler Spanner Wrench	EA	1
Tow Bar, Aluminum Torsion	EA	1

Trailer, Twin Axle 25'
    Load Capacity 8,000 Lbs
    Weight 2,000 Lbs.
    Length Overall 27'5"
    Width Overall 96"
    Tire Size 8/14.51' (4)
    Tire, Size 8/14.51' (Spare)
    Winch Capacity 3,200 Lbs.
	EA	1

Transom Cap, Stainless Steel	EA	1
Trim Tabs, Hydraulic	EA	2
Trim Tabs, Power Unit (Bennet)	EA	2
Trim Tilt, Motor & Cable	EA	2
Weapons, Rifle Holder/Rack	EA	1

Appendix E
25' TPSB CHECK OFF LISTS

Overview

Introduction	This appendix are standard boat check off list.

THIS PAGE LEFT INTENTIONALLY BLANK

Underway Checklist (25' Transportable Port Security Boat)

Boat # _____   Trailer # _____   Date: _____   Time: _____

Coxswain _____   Engineer: _____

Boat Crew: _____   Boat Crew: _____

Other: _____   Other: _____

Other: _____   Other: _____

EQUIPMENT (BOW TO STERN)

Forward Sump (Scuttle)

Boat Plug			
Gun Mount			
Anchor Locker			
Anchor-Danforth			
Anchor Line (150')			
Anchor Chain (5')			
Bilge Pump			

Coxswain Console

Fire Extinguisher			
Spot Light			
GPS			
Compass			
AN/PRC-117 (Radio)			
Fathometer			
Radar			
VHF-FM Radio			
Kill Switch			
Loudhailer w/ Microphone			

Leaning Post Stowage

Air-horn			
Binoculars			
Chart (s)			
Kill Switch (spare)			
Navigation Kit			
Pyro Can			

Fuel Status (circle)   Full   ¾   1/2
                                      ¼   0

Oil (circle)   Full   ¾   1/2
                             ¼   0

Aft Area

Boat Hook (Stbd)					
Boat Plug (Stbd)					
Bilge Pump (Stbd)					
Fenders (4)					
Flagstaff					
Flag – U. S.					
Flag – Coast Guard					
Gun Mounts (2)					
Life Ring					
Mooring Lines					
Paddles (2)					
Rescue Heaving Line					
PFD Bag					
PFD (5), Type III					
Survival Vests					
Knife					
MK-79 Pencil Flare Kit					
Mirror (Signal)					
MK-124 (Day/Night Flare)					
Strobe (SDU-5)					
Whistle					
PML (Chem-Lite)					
Propellers					
5-Gallon Bucket					

Overall

Antennas (5)				
Cleats (7)				
Rub-Rails				
VHF Antenna Raised				

Remarks:

_____

_____

_____

_____

Engineer Log (25' Transportable Port Security Boat)

Boat # _____   Trailer # _____   Date: _____   Time: _____

Engineer:

_____

	Engine Number	Hour Meters Start	Stop
Port			
Starboard			

BEFORE OPERATION

Fluids:	Fuel:	¼	½	¾	Full	Quantity Added:	_____
	Oil (Stbd)	¼	½	¾	Full	Quantity Added:	_____
	Oil (Port)	¼	½	¾	Full	Quantity Added:	_____

Sat	Unsat	Trailer
		Bow Safety Hook/Chain
		Hitch/Wiring Harness/Chains
		Lights (Brake/Blinker/Side)
		Lug Nuts
		Rollers/Side Rails
		Tires/Spare
		Trailer Jack
		Winch/Strap/Hook

Hull

Sat	Unsat	
		Bilge Pumps
		Bulwarks
		Cleats/Guards/Hardware
		Deck Openings
		Drain Plugs
		Exterior/Rub Rails
		Fuel Tank Vent/Cap
		Mechanical Fuel Gauge
		Overall Condition

Engines

Sat	Unsat	
		Cables/Lines/Linkages
		Engine Mounts/Transom
		Propellers
		Tilt/Trim Operation

Lights

Sat	Unsat	
		Blue Strobe (Console/mast)
		Navigation (Port/Stbd/Mast)
		Spotlight

Sat	Unsat	Console
		Batteries
		Cables/Terminal Blocks/Wires
		Circuit Breakers/Fuses
		Gauges/Switches
		Antenna/Power Connections
		Batteries
		Compass
		Fathometer
		Gauges/Switches
		GPS
		Loudhailer
		Overall Condition
		An/ PRC-117
		Radar
		Steering
		Throttles
		Trim Tab Fluid Level
		VHF-FM Radio

Tower

Sat	Unsat	
		Antennas
		Mounting Hardware
		Radar Dome
		Transom
		Battery Cables
		Fuel Filters
		Fuel Lines
		Oil Lines
		VRO Oil Tanks

UNDERWAY CHECKS

Sat	Unsat	Operation
		Bilge Pumps
		Electronics

Sat	Unsat	Engines
		Alarms/Warnings
		General Operations

Gauge's Operations
Steering
Throttle Operation
Trim Tab Operation

Oil Pressure
Propellers
Temperature
Tilt/Trim
Water Pumps

Remarks: _____

www.ingramcontent.com/pod-product-compliance
Lightning Source LLC
Chambersburg PA
CBHW081832280526

45789CB00007B/2437